Maths all Week

a BEAM Education sourcebook

June Loewenstein

BEAM Education

BEAM Education is a specialist mathematics education publisher, dedicated to promoting the teaching and learning of mathematics as interesting, challenging and enjoyable.

BEAM materials cover teaching and learning needs from the age of 3 to 14. They deal with many of the classroom concerns voiced by teachers of mathematics, and offer practical support and help. BEAM materials include more than 80 publications, as well as a comprehensive range of mathematical games and equipment.

BEAM services include consultancy for companies, institutions and government, and a programme of courses and in-service training for schools, early years settings and local education authorities.

BEAM is an acknowledged expert in the field of mathematics education.

BEAM Education
Maze Workshops
72a Southgate Road
London N1 3JT
info@beam.co.uk

Orders:
orderline 01242 267945
beamorders@nelsonthornes.com
www.beam.co.uk

Published by BEAM Education
© BEAM Education 2003
All rights reserved.
ISBN 1 874099 97 9
British Library Cataloguing-in-Publication Data
Data available
Edited by Nicola Liu
Designed by Jenny Buzzard
Photography includes the work of Len Cross and Sally Greenhill
Workshop featured on pages 8-9: Architecture Workshops (www.awa.ndo.co.uk)

Typeset by BEAM Education
Printed in Scotland by Scotprint

Foreword

It's unusual in our culture to celebrate mathematics, but that's what a Maths Week is about. The aim is to create buzz, excitement, and intellectual stimulation and rigour. We want to hear children say 'I love maths!' and to see them relish the mental gymnastics that true mathematical activity affords. The hope is that the success of 'maths all week' will convert it into 'maths all year'.

Many schools have embarked on this process; we are indebted to them for passing on their experience and wisdom, and sharing with us the joyfulness of mathematics as play, comedy, and tough thinking. Our thanks go in particular to the staff and children of the Blue Coat School, the Holy Ghost RC Primary School, Prior Weston Primary School and Streatham Wells Primary School for their help. Thanks also to Carole Booth and Angelika Bradley for their expertise, and to Jenny Buzzard and Nicola Liu for all their hard work. Most of all, we are grateful to the many teachers who said they needed a book like this, and to June Loewenstein for putting her time, energy and writing skills to work on the task.

Sheila Ebbutt
BEAM Education

Contents

Case studies

Architecture and construction

This is an inner-city primary school. They run a Maths and Science Week each year, and always use this as an opportunity to set the curriculum aside for that one week in the year. Their Maths and Science Week was held in November, and the theme was 'Architecture and construction'.

Back in the classroom

Different exercises and investigations had been planned ahead of time, to give children practice in applying problem-solving skills. One project was farm-based and involved designing a dairy product. Another was to design and construct an animal carrier (and to provide the model animal for it). Some of this work was done at home, to involve the families.

Out and about

Throughout the Week different Year groups walked the city streets looking at selected buildings, visiting some of them, and sketching their shape and architectural features. The children looked at contemporary and old buildings, discussed the function of the buildings and reinforced their observations with trips to museums and local sites of architectural excellence. The lower school looked for signs of how animals are housed in city buildings and went to the local zoo to study housing styles used there.

Workshops and challenges

Toward the end of the Week the school held its regular Open Evening. The activities included an architecture workshop and a challenge (for adults and children) to design and build an item of furniture out of newspaper.

Bringing in the adults

The school's philosophy is one of collaboration and enthusiastic endeavour. During the Open Evening parents and other family members moved throughout the school, joining in set activities and experiments, working with the children to find out the results and to construct models, towers and pyramids together. Adults got down on their knees and joined in the fun.

Making maths fun

This is a small suburban primary school, and this was their first attempt at a Maths Week. The timetable allowed for some regular classes to continue, in between Maths Week activities for the whole school. The Maths Week was held in March, and the theme was 'Making maths fun' – for everyone, including parents and staff.

Monday

The Maths Week began with an assembly for the whole school. Children were given a differentiated investigation and asked to complete it by the end of the day. They had to work out how many octopuses and mermaids were swimming in the sea, based on eye-witness data (28 arms, 10 tails and 22 eyes) and the information that octopuses have eight arms and mermaids have two arms and a tail. Older children were asked extension questions, such as 'what if there were 100 eyes?'.

The Monday assembly also set in motion a project designed to run through the Week. The children were given a budget (to cover resources like scissors, stars and gold pens) and invited to design and make a maths game.

Tuesday

Hattie the Maths Clown spent the day at the school. She blew bubbles, made number patterns, threw balls with different number operations on for the children to catch, and told jokes and tricks.

In between sessions with Hattie and their regular classes, the children continued working on their maths games.

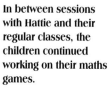

Wednesday

The children brought in quizzes that they had been working on at home.

During the morning the children up to Year 2 went (in batches) to a workshop on measures, shape and space. Parents came in to help facilitate. Each class was divided into five groups. Each group went from table to table, weighing teddies and torches, creating symmetrical patterns with pegboards, constructing cuboids and triangular prisms, and measuring the width of the room and the height of the stool.

At the same time, the children in Years 3 to 6 were in the hall, taking part in a team-based maths competition. The questions were graded in difficulty, to allow all the children a chance of succeeding, and different categories were devised, so that more than one team could win.

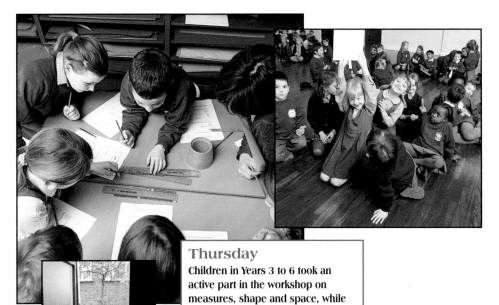

Thursday

Children in Years 3 to 6 took an active part in the workshop on measures, shape and space, while the younger children battled fiercely in their own maths competition.

Friday

At a final assembly the headteacher announced the different team winners of the competition and the quiz. Then the children were given free rein to play the games that they had been working on all week. Older children paired up with younger ones to test out the games. The best were later laminated and displayed.

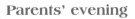

Parents' evening

Many people came early to the parents' evening, to sample the maths books and games stalls. Some volunteered, for a bit of fun, to put themselves in their children's shoes and try out some test papers usually given to the children. The evening ended with a presentation by teachers and pupils, explaining the school's approach to teaching maths.

Maths all around you

This infant school (attached to a larger school) is in a semi-rural part of the country. This was their first go at a Maths Week. Planning started six months beforehand. The school's aims included 'reinforcing children's view that maths is exciting' and 'placing maths in a wider context', and the theme was 'Mathematics all around you'. The Maths Week was held in June.

Maths in books

Children practised counting and number recognition when they read 'The three little wolves and the big bad pig', 'There's no such thing as a dragon' and 'The patchwork cat'. They also worked on shape, size and pattern. After reading 'Penguins in the fridge', they made up their own penguin puzzles and constructed penguins of their own design for a number frieze.

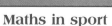

Maths in sport

One of the aims was to apply maths to different curriculum areas – including sport. As part of this, children plotted their own time and distance experiments: how many easy jumps could they do in ten seconds? and in one minute? and how about bench hops? how far could they leap from one leg? how far could they go if they did three jumps from a standing position? Then they carried out these experiments and recorded their findings. Back in the classroom, they used spreadsheets to analyse the data and compare results.

Maths in food

Children baked chocolate chip cookies and served them up in a café. Extra batches were made and frozen, for use in Open Afternoons the following week. They also found out how rice is grown and calculated how much rice is needed to feed a family for a week.

Maths in art

Children worked on shape, size and pattern. They made tablecloths, classroom displays and fabulous maths hats.

Maths in the environment

Children went on a Maths Trail in the school environment. Different Year groups did different parts of the Trail. Questions included:

Where can you see patterns with squares? [and] with rectangles? What happens at the edges of the pattern? Try and draw the pattern.

What shape are the fence posts? Try and draw them.

How many trees with white bark can you see at the end of the playground? What are these trees called?

Where can you see a circle and lots of spheres?

How many black-framed windows are there? How many panes of glass [are there] in each window? How many panes of glass are there altogether?'

Spend 5 minutes doing a traffic survey. In different groups you could count a) how many cars turn into school, b) how many cars turn right at the traffic lights…

In their evaluation session, the teachers decided to repeat the Trail next time, because it had worked so well, but to make it shorter and clearer (by separating the questions from the instructions).

Mathematics at large

This is a medium-sized primary school with a history of successful Book Weeks and Music Weeks. Their aims in introducing a Maths Week were to 'build confidence in maths' and to 'help children appreciate mathematics at work in the real world'. The Maths Week was held in June.

Countdown

In the weeks running up to the Maths Week, the children were given a maths problem to take home each Friday. During the weekend families worked to find solutions to challenges such as 'How may different three-scoop ice-cream cones can you make from five different kinds of ice cream?' and 'Can you make a Palindrome number?' The whole school seemed to be discussing maths problems. All the different contributions were displayed in the entrance hall and prizes were awarded to all the children who had taken part.

The Maths Coordinator told parents about the forthcoming Maths Week in the letter that was sent out with the homework.

Outings

All the children visited a nearby museum to see the 'Number Crunching' exhibition. Most classes also took part in a Maths Trail in the local park or went on a Number Walk round local streets.

Assemblies

The Monday assembly was used to tell the children about the Maths Week activities, games and trips out of school. The Friday assembly was taken by Year 6. They had written a script for a radio programme on the theme of mathematics. The quizzes, songs, jokes and reports all focused on mathematics.

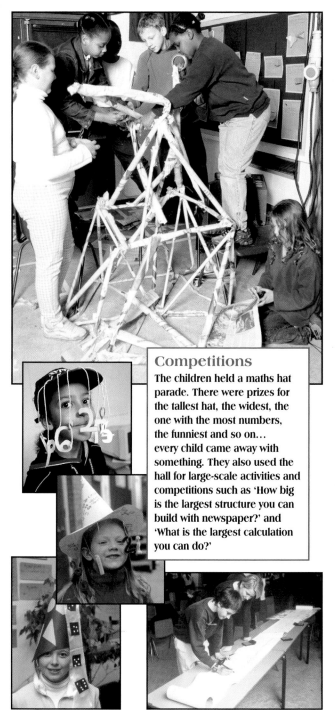

Shops

The children ordered mathematical materials, worked out a pricing structure and set up a Maths Shop. A year later, the school's bookshop was still getting requests for mathematical materials.

Competitions

The children held a maths hat parade. There were prizes for the tallest hat, the widest, the one with the most numbers, the funniest and so on… every child came away with something. They also used the hall for large-scale activities and competitions such as 'How big is the largest structure you can build with newspaper?' and 'What is the largest calculation you can do?'

Games

One class used the playground to organise sports activities and to try out games of their own design. They worked out all the rules, then chalked the game up on the playground surface and invited other classes to take part. They used charts to record the scores.

Planning

use the Maths Week to
capitalise on colleagues' particular strengths, **focus on lesser-known topics,** generate enthusiasm, **work on long-term projects, tackle specific needs, place mathematics in the real world,** make connections, involve the parents, integrate the curriculum, **think out of the box**

Getting started

In your role as maths coordinator, the first thing to do to get your Maths Week under way is enlist the support of the headteacher (and possibly also the governing body). Prepare an outline plan before you introduce the idea to the head (and, in a large school, the senior management team). Include in your plan the particular benefits to the school of holding a Maths Week. This early meeting may also be a good time to discuss budgets and provisional dates. The next thing is to win the support of colleagues when you tell them your idea at a staff meeting. Choose a slot when you know that people will have time and energy for a discussion. Distribute your outline plan and then, as a way of involving everyone from the start, brainstorm some ideas. Agree a definite date: make it at least a term ahead, maybe longer. And check your budget. Is it clear who has control over it? Are the figures realistic? Finally, invite your colleagues to join a small planning group. (Invite everyone, even if you already know who you wish to have in the group.) This group will meet several times to put together the detailed plan that will go to the staff and head for approval.

A Maths Week can

add to children's pleasure in mathematics

place mathematics in a wider context

raise standards across the curriculum

be an opportunity for staff development

strengthen links with the community

inspire children and their teachers

Action points

Agree on your aims and write these down.

Keep it simple by choosing just a few aims. If you achieve more than you set out to do, see it as a bonus. Discuss criteria that you can use to measure your success. How will you recognise whether you have succeeded in your aims?

Decide on the format.

Will all classes be involved? Key Stage 1 only? Year 6 only? Do you want to run the Maths Week over a series of individual Maths Days, spread over a term or the year? Will you have an open day on Thursday, with a maths fair in the evening? Would it be better to do this a week after the event, to allow time to prepare and to enable you to focus on the needs of the Week itself without being distracted?

Select one or more themes.

Themes are not mandatory but they do provide a focus and give a feeling of coherence and purpose to the week. Be mindful of colleagues' strengths and their interests. If you have teachers who are passionate about art, the environment or history, consider using these as themes. If nobody is strong on music, don't try to make this the week you get to grips with it.

Draw up a list of possible activities.

Use the brainstorm from the staff meeting as a starting-point. Decide whether you want to link these to Curriculum-based learning objectives (you don't have to), and if so, what those should be.

Review the school timetable.

Check what teaching sessions or visits are fixed, and plan around these. Consider whether it's possible (or desirable) to incorporate these in the Maths Week.

Allocate tasks.

Decide who does what in your planning group and what specific jobs you could ask other staff to do. For instance, you may want to video the parents' evening, or order some maths books and equipment on sale-or-return for a maths shop – these are concrete tasks that could be done by someone not on the group.

Discuss possible guests or visitors.

Draw up a short-list, decide priorities and agree who will contact guests to find out whether and when they are available. Arrange for someone (the same person?) to be responsible for all communication with the visitor and to support them where appropriate.

Make a note to keep people informed.

Tell the premises officer well in advance (or others involved in the use of the building) about any evenings when the school needs to stay open, about extra use of the hall or other facilities, extra chairs, and so on.

Review your financial resources.

Produce a plan showing how you are allocating funds and how the money will be spent. Allow for contingencies and plan ahead about reporting back after the event. Consider whether there is scope for any fundraising or need for parental involvement.

Review your non-financial resources.

Think about material and equipment resources such as the OHPs, playground or computer room and discuss how to share these between the classes. Think about people resources too, and how to make the best use of these: teaching assistants, part-time staff, parents… You may need to reorganise the timetable for teaching assistants. You may want to invite, or buy in, extra help (perhaps the music teacher for an extra half-day or a governor); this could need booking well in advance.

Consider the children.

Decide when to tell the children and whether to involve them in the planning.

Aims

have a chance to try new things

reinforce the idea that maths can be fun

develop thinking skills

harness creativity

forge links with the community

put your school on the map

share the curriculum with parents

provide in-service training

raise funds for the school

broaden the mathematics curriculum

make links with other curriculum areas

foster an additional language

give children the chance to work in a new setting

Themes

food

investigations

mazes

movement

pattern

time

sport

maths and art

maths and science

maths and design

maths and citizenship

maths and the environment

maths and music

maths and games

maths from around the world

put mathematics to work

shape and size

structures

the past, present and future of mathematics

where we are

or

maths all week:

maths in art (Mon)

maths in books (Tue)

maths at home (Wed)

maths in music (Thur)

maths in food (Fri)

Delegating

When you introduce your draft plan to the whole staff, keep your written document to just a few pages and think beforehand about contingency planning, so that you know how to respond if people start coming up with problems. Present your plan confidently: if you appear uncertain, you might have to make more changes than you need, entailing further discussion and more planning time. Be open to new ideas, but remember that you are aiming not for perfection but for a quality Week: don't be wary of deciding to put good ideas on hold for another year.

And delegate! Produce your list of tasks and pass them round (to everyone, headteacher and non-teaching staff alike). Decide early on which events, outings or activities require special treatment and allocate responsibility to specific individuals.

Tasks for the planning group

Someone in the planning group will need to create a timetable, allocating activities, special events, whole-school gatherings and class assemblies, based on the resources available. Decide also who should specify and order in any material resources, for use that week only or also for longer-term use.

It's important to keep people informed. A progress chart or similar device can be a quick and easy way to keep people up to date. Arrange also for someone to contact parents and ask for help if you need it, now and nearer the date. At the same time, they can enlist the support of the governors. Someone else can sort out visitors and guest speakers; you'll want to be clear on who is going to visit the school and for how long. The same person can contact the visitors to make provisional and then final bookings ahead of time.

The brief will include

aims

dates

theme

suggested activities

visitors

outings

special events

a budget resumé

Progress chart

To do	Who	When	What	Funding
Timetables	Mike	end of half term	consult	
Letter to parents	Sarah Joyce	wk ending 15 Jan	letter typed photocopied	
Survey of plants with Wildlife Trust	Rashid	wk ending 15 Jan	ring Trust: agree date and ask for pack	
	Liam	today	ask for 2 parent helpers	
	Tina and Liam	by end Feb	plan activities based on pack	
	Rashid	by end Feb	tell Trust what has been done	
Artist's visit	Annie	wk ending 15 Jan	talk to class teachers involved	£250
	Annie	wk ending 22 Jan	initial call to artist	
	Annie	by beg Feb	ring artist to brief and agree on fee	
	Tina	wk ending 12 Feb	check timetable for availability of hall	
	Annie	by end Feb	confirm booking	
Premises officer	Mike	tomorrow	tell Ted	
Maths team at teachers centre	Susan	by beg Feb	speak re contribution to staff meeting + workshops + parents evening	
Ask Turkish deli	Liu Tang	Friday	check out possibility of a visit	
Class resources	Planning group	wk ending 22 Jan	survey needs	£500
	Tina	meeting on 25 Jan by beg Feb	collate resources order extra resources	

Special events

— a Maths Walk or Trail

— a Maths shop, auction or bring-and-buy sale

— a café for parents and/or children

— a visitor for the whole school, or for younger children in the morning and older ones in the afternoon

— different visitors for different classes

— a visit to a science museum, an art gallery, a park, the seaside, the high street, a fire station...

— outings in the immediate school environment

— a maths master class run by a local university

— a fundraising marathon

— an Open Day or Evening

— a Maths and Sports Day

Making it special

One school chose Maths and Science as its theme. During planning, the teachers of Years 5 and 6 decided to make a hot air balloon with the children and launch it during the Week.

— Planning
A few weeks beforehand, the teachers worked with their classes to brainstorm the maths and science involved. They discussed the balloon's shape and size, the materials and equipment needed, where to obtain helium, the optimal weather conditions, and health and safety issues. One child thought of contacting the local balloon club for advice. Someone else suggested surfing the Internet. They made an action plan from all the ideas, and found an area in the school playground where large-scale work could be carried out. The children used reference books and websites to get more information. An enthusiast from the local balloon club agreed to visit the school.

— Design
At the start of the Week, the children explored the maths involved in the design. They developed designs of nets for balloon shapes, used tissue paper to experiment on a small scale, and held a vote to agree a design. Next, one set worked out the number of sections and their correct size, including overlap. They wrote instructions with specs for children to work from. Other sets worked on the lettering to go on the balloon's surface; they checked the weather forecast for the launch day; and estimated how far the balloon might travel given wind direction, and where it might land.

— Construction
With the help of the local ballooning enthusiast, the children cut and stuck sections together in groups and made the balloon. They attached a label, for safe retrieval.

— Launch
On launch day the whole school gathered on the playground to watch proudly as the balloon caught the wind. Two children, with a teacher, followed it through the streets and retrieved it from a field about a kilometre away.

— Evaluation
The children discussed the merits of the project, what they had learned and how it could have been even better.

Organising

It will help to map out beforehand the resources you will need, so that you have time enough to buy in equipment that will outlive the Maths Week (if you have the budget) and time in which to enlist the support of people in making props or volunteering for help during outings. Many of your decisions will be based on simple logistics: who needs to be in the Hall when, how many children will fit into the staff room, how many helpers will be needed for science experiments, and so forth. Time, money and people are all valuable resources. People, in particular, can be very helpful, if only to suggest ways of stretching your budget and making the most of your time. Ask for ideas: they may be all you need.

Use the intangibles

imagination

generosity

intelligence

dedication

humour

efficiency

Resources

— time

— money

— people
  teaching staff, support staff, parents and friends, school governors, local community, children

— equipment
  computers, OHP, interactive whiteboard, cooking materials, oven, art materials, musical instruments

— space
  the Hall, playground, and so on

— local spaces

Playground (Maths Week activities)

Hall (Maths Week activities)

Staff room (Maths Week cooking activities)

	Monday	Tuesday	Wednesday	Thursday	Friday
		assistant: Joey	assistant: Joey	assistant: Joey	
10 – 11		Year 3 (group A)	Year 4 (group A)	Year 5 (group B)	
11 – 12		Year 3 (group B)	Year 4 (group B)	Year 5 (group C)	
	dinner				
	assistant: Simon	assistant: Simon	assistant: parents		
1.15 – 2.15	Year 6 (group A)	Year 3 (group C)	Year 4 (group C)		
2.15 – 3.15	Year 6 (group B)	Year 6 (group C)	Year 5 (group A)		

Outline planning

One school created resource zones, where space, people and equipment were set aside to cater for the needs of pupils working on different areas of the curriculum. The content and activities were selected to reflect the school aims, to pick up on specific areas of the curriculum and to draw on teachers' particular enthusiasms. Teachers created their own lesson plans using outline resource timetables and ideas taken from an activity sheet.

Resources activity sheet

art and design (pink zone)
— printing challenges (repeated patterns, overlaps, symmetrical patterns, tiling patterns)
— weaving challenges (paper looms, sheep's wool weaving, non-symmetrical weaving)
— folding paper (stars, origami, folding and cutting)
— enlarging and copying prints of famous paintings
— computer graphics and Logo
— sculptures from found objects to fit in a measured space.

music (blue zone)
— number songs and rhymes (tapes and CDs)
— repeating rhythm patterns
— composing and recording music on computer
— inventing music notation
— pitch with bottle gongs and metal chimes
— circle games
— square dancing.

design and technology (orange zone)
— designing and making a bird table
— making a recipe for a bird cake
— designing and making a kite
— investigating how kites fly
— designing and making a sundial
— investigating shadows throughout the day
— designing and making a wind machine
— measuring wind force, or the force of a breath
— evaluating how gardening tools work.

science (purple zone, and green outdoor zone)
— data-handling project (the wildlife garden)
— making collections from the local surroundings
— sorting, classifying and arranging collections
— making and using classification keys
— using hoops to do a ground survey
— identifying local animals and plants
— comparing habitats
— weather survey (rain, wind, sun)
— observing the bird table and collecting data
— investigating food chains
— investigating shapes, patterns and symmetry in plants
— using databases on computer
— using a computer-based encyclopaedia.

English (red zone, and Hall)
— produce an audio tape of the Maths Trail
— number rhymes, counting books, puzzle books
— storytellings from books with a maths theme
— reading (with Years 5 and 6) *The Phantom Tollbooth* and discussing it
— mathematical poetry writing: poems with numbers, haiku, visual poetry with a shape
— debate on our food: read arguments for and against organic farming
— writing contributions to the Maths Week journal
— inventing a mathematical board game and writing the rules down.

physical education (green outdoor zone, and Hall)
— creating and performing repeated movement patterns and shapes
— making different shapes with the whole body
— inventing games in small groups using small apparatus, and recording the rules
— using a fitness circuit with a set number of challenges
— orienteering round the school and fields.

Agreeing the detail

When you start on your final planning, remember that individual teachers will probably want control over the activities they use and the structure of the Week for their class. Resourcing has to be agreed from the outset, and your aims need to be clear to everyone. But after that, it can be left up to the teachers to choose and plan their activities. The different approaches include taking a mathematical topic as a springboard and then brainstorming where to go from there; or choosing as your starting point a topic from elsewhere in the curriculum and then identifying the maths within that area; or doing a study of mathematics right across the curriculum. Detailed planning can be shared if that's a help to the team; if it isn't, then keep the basic structure in mind and let individuals do their own thing.

Don't forget

keep some things in reserve

give individual teachers flexibility

communicate ideas to get shared ownership

experiment (in small doses)

involve the children

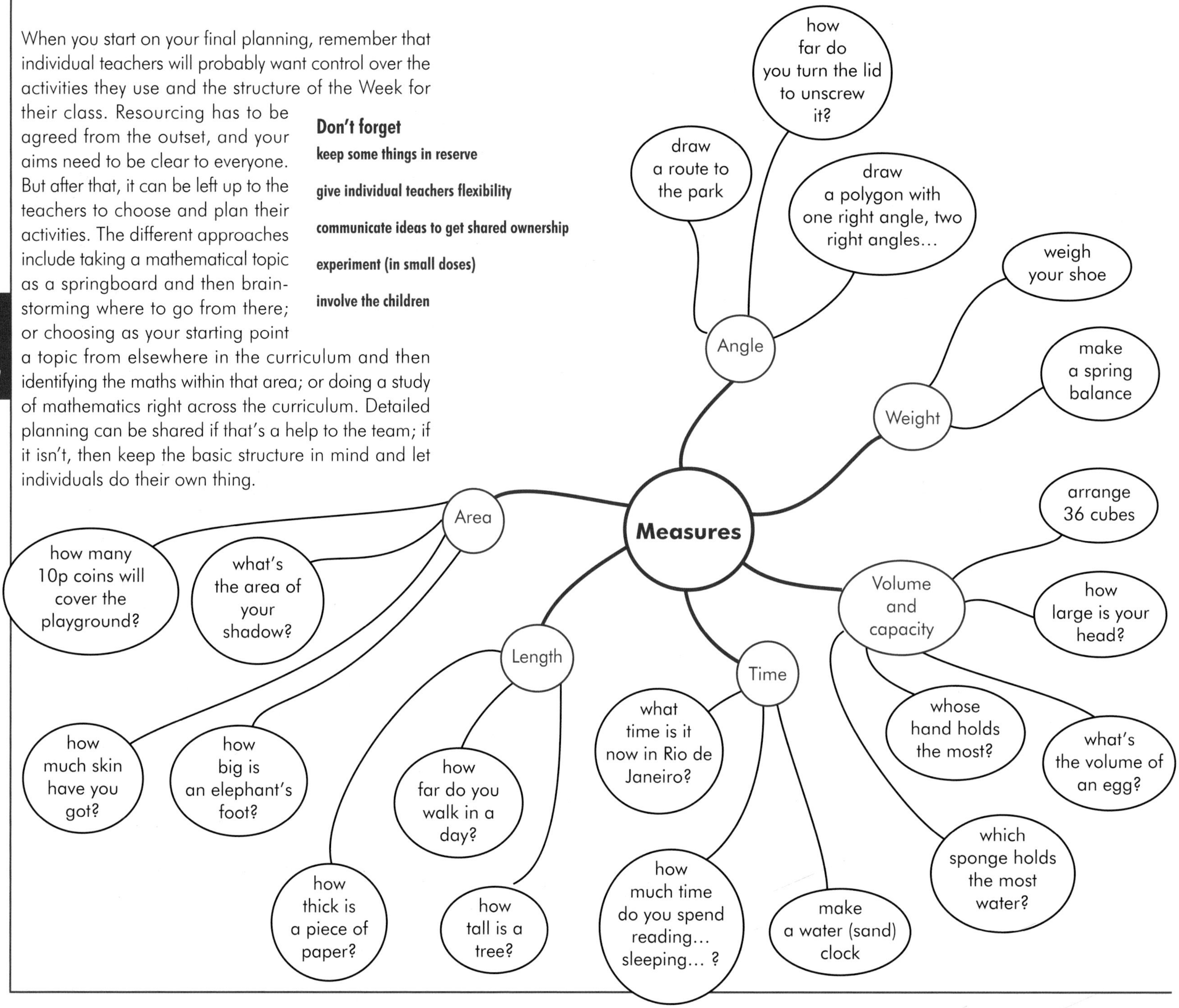

24

Measures

Angle
- how far do you turn the lid to unscrew it?
- draw a route to the park
- draw a polygon with one right angle, two right angles…

Weight
- weigh your shoe
- make a spring balance

Area
- how many 10p coins will cover the playground?
- what's the area of your shadow?

Volume and capacity
- arrange 36 cubes
- how large is your head?
- whose hand holds the most?
- what's the volume of an egg?
- which sponge holds the most water?

Length
- how much skin have you got?
- how big is an elephant's foot?
- how far do you walk in a day?
- how thick is a piece of paper?
- how tall is a tree?

Time
- what time is it now in Rio de Janeiro?
- how much time do you spend reading… sleeping… ?
- make a water (sand) clock

Mathematics from other curriculum areas

Geography
- local geography: map of the area, A to Z (position, measures)
- fieldwork in local environment: the cemetery, River Street, Kearsney Abbey (position, measures, angle)
- sustainability in the local environment (data handling)
- change in local land use (number, data handling)

English
- describing, talking and writing about maths problems (communication, vocabulary)
- using mathematical language appropriately (communication, vocabulary)
- listening to talks and presentations (communication)
- group discussions (communication)
- reading mathematical stories and poems (solving problems)
- reading and writing word problems (solving problems)

History
- local history: story of the mills, canal (dates and changes over time)
- timeline of place events, people and changes (time)
- dates relating to the passing of time (time)
- selecting and organising historical information (data handling)
- history of mathematics and mathematicians

Science
- animals and plants in the school environment (data handling)
- grouping and classifying materials (data handling)
- electricity, forces, light and sound (measurement in experiments)
- sun, earth and moon (distances and periodic changes)

Art and design
- relationship between 2D and 3D designs (shape and space)
- rotation, reflection and translation in print making (position and movement)
- enlarging paintings and images (position and movement)
- computer graphics (shape and space)

PE
- creating and performing dances using movement patterns (number patterns, position and movement)
- making up and playing small-sided games (problem solving, position and movement)
- analysing rules and conventions for different activities (data handling)
- fitness and health (number, measures, data handling)

Music
- counting songs and rhymes
- movement and dance and investigation into shape of body and use of space (3D shape, position and movement)
- counting and recording rhythms (number patterns)
- using computers to change and combine sounds (number patterns)
- recording timed sequences (number, time)

ICT
- finding information from the internet (data handling)
- using computer software to explore geometry (2D shape, angle)
- presenting results using computer software (number, data handling)
- playing computer maths games and puzzles (problem solving)

Design and technology
- planning and making models (2D and 3D space)
- cooking (measures)
- investigating and analysing tools and how they work (position and movement)
- print making (symmetry, position and movement)

Taking a different view

It's entirely up to you how you run your Maths Week. Experience, confidence and resources will all play a part in the decisions that you make when you're planning the Week. Just remember that you can do as you please this week. You can split the Week into Maths Days. You can put the Curriculum (or National Guidelines) on one side for these five days. You can take one investigation and set the whole school to work on it. You can select any curriculum area and explore the mathematics that underpins it. You can take large subjects and arrange for children to present their findings in a public arena (to parents in the school hall, as part of an exhibition in the local library or at a stall in your shopping centre or market square). You can use all or part of the Week to focus on the transition to secondary school for Year 6 children. You can create a timetable that allows maths-based activities to take place in one part of the school for some of the children and the normal timetable to continue in another part for the rest. You can have artists in residence, storytellers in residence, poets in residence, even scientists… . You can make links with local theatres or universities or companies. You can create schemes that may live on beyond the Week, like a maths club or a magazine or a Number Partners programme in the community. You really can do anything you please, whether modest, ambitious or somewhere in the middle.

Consider

holding separate Maths Days

combining Maths Week with Book Week

mounting a Week-long investigation

holding an Open Event the following week

combining Maths Week with a whole-school outing

combining Maths Week for one Year group with a school trip

Splitting the Week

One school held their Maths Week over a series of five Maths Days, one each half term for the first two terms and then one in the Summer term.

— Targeting one Year group

The school decided to focus on one Year group for this experimental first year, and chose Year 5.

— Developing financial capability

The theme was 'Money' (financial capability). All the activities aimed to reinforce the children's grasp of financial understanding, financial competence and financial responsibility.

— Emphasising citizenship

Because the school prioritises PSHE and good citizenship, they emphasized this in the timetable and scheduled in opportunities for debate and voting. This approach linked with the school aim of encouraging thinking skills and educating children to see the bigger picture. The Maths Week focused on giving to charity and included fundraising activities for a charity selected by the children. One fundraising event was the Spring Fair, held at the end of the fourth Maths Day.

— Caring for the environment

Another priority was a concern for the school environment. Hence the tub garden idea. This project included repaying a debt and buying plants from the nearest garden centre.

— Setting project work

The first four Maths Days ended with ongoing projects. This kept the momentum between Maths Days.

— Closing the Week

The Week ended in a school assembly, with a presentation to family and friends, a report on the fundraising campaign and the distribution of material from the Week for children to keep at home.

Autumn term (1)	Autumn term (2)	Spring term (1)	Spring term (2)	Summer term
financial understanding	**financial competence**	**financial responsibility**		
registration	registration	registration	registration	registration
assembly	assembly	assembly	assembly	(75) Cooking: prepare café
(60) Poster: history and future of money	(60) Saving for a purpose: giving to a charity	(45) Breakfast at school: Activity: cost the breakfast	(60) Prepare Spring Fair	
	Plan Spring Fair and other sponsored activities	(30) Plan Spring Fair and other activities		
break	break	break	break	break
(15) Discussion: where money comes from	(25) Saving for a purpose: giving gifts	(30) Plan Spring Fair	(115) Garden centre trip	(40) Café
(60) Activity: Job centre	Activity: catalogue pages	(40) Activity: National Savings		(20) Check money books
(40) Visitors: my job (profiles)	Activities: (45) Internet books (30) gift token or voucher	(45) Songs Circle time: needs, wants Write a song		
	(15) Circle time: setting a limit on cost of gifts			
lunch then registration	lunch then registration	lunch then registration	lunch then registration	lunch then registration
(15) Discussion: where money goes	(60) Saving for a purpose: brightening up the school	(60) Activity: cost of living (using Jacqueline Wilson book)	(30) Plant tub garden	(45) Report on all activities
(45) Activity: choose a birthday present	Plan tub garden; borrow money			(20) Check money books
break	break	break	break	break
(40) Circle time: giving to charity	(40) Activity: Job Centre (job interviews)	(25) Prepare	(40) Prepare Spring Fair	(15) Prepare
Brainstorm ideas; secret vote		(15) Year 5 assembly		(25) Assembly presentation
plenary	plenary	plenary	plenary	plenary
			(40) **Spring Fair**	
Project 1) Create your own catalogue page	Project 1) Read JW book 2) Chores for charity	Project 1) Prepare Spring Fair 2) Chores for charity	Project 1) Find a recipe 2) Chores for charity	

(30) **approximate time per session**

Creating a Maths Trail

A Maths Trail is an excellent way to involve children in their learning – not to mention the friends and family who visit the school during Maths Week. There are as many different ways to organise one as there are schools. A good Maths Trail needs some questions that the children can answer immediately and some that entail collecting materials to take back to the classroom for follow-up work.

Decide early on whether to hold the Maths Trail as an event, with children or staff managing it, or to run it as a self-directed activity, using a Maths Trail activity sheet that people can fill in at any time in the Week. If you have never done one before, make sure you time the route and visualise how it will work. Keep it simple. Aim to motivate the children and to include relevant mathematical content.

Topic-based questions can cover 'time', 'number', 'calculating', 'shape', 'data', and so on. (Bear in mind the varying needs of children, based on their level and preferred style of learning.)

The logistics involved in moving that number of children around will not be new to you, but think about how you can enable them all to stop at times and examine something closely. Make sure there are enough adult helpers for the younger children.

Think also about follow-up. How can you use this data? Can you display the material children have brought back? Is there a maths game the children can make out of this? Or a visual diary or similar record? Can you modify and then keep the Maths Trail as a maths tool for future use? Or would the children like to be involved in writing a new trail (lasting anything from ten minutes to half an hour)? Remember that any place can be a focus for a Maths Trail and primary children of any age can participate.

A Maths Trail will

locate maths in the real world

encourage children to observe

give children problems to solve

yield data for classroom activities

give children exercise

Our school Maths Trail

An adult and child staffed each stop on the trail and had the next clue, on coloured slips, ready to hand out to seekers who identified the trail item correctly – and who could hold up the slip from the previous stop. (This meant that clues were solved in the correct order.) The trail started in the library with a red clue. At the end, everyone who completed the trail won a filled balloon.

— Red clue

Go to the cloakroom and look at the floor.
Read the number there and add 10 more.
(number chalked on floor)

— Blue clue

Go to the playground, near the swing, and once you are there, look for the games that are played on the ground, and count the squares.
(squares in hopscotch grid)

...

This Maths Trail was made by Year 6

Answer all 20 questions and put your name on the sheet. The first sheet we take from the box with all answers correct will win a Mystery Prize.

— Outside of building

1 Find a date between 1800 and 2000. Where is it?

2 How many gates are in the south-facing playground wall?

3 What is below the round window?

— School hall

1 What shape are the windows above the stage?

2 How many red hoops are there?

3 Are the benches 1·83 metres long or 8·31 metres long?

4 How many circles can you see on the wall to the left of the stage?

5 ...

A Maths Trail on different levels

One school organised a Maths Trail from the school, round a local park, to some shops and back to school. The teacher planned the trail for three different levels of difficulty so that all age groups could take part.

Maths Trail A

1. Count how many poles there are on the way down the slope.
2. Multiply the numbers in the phone number on the portable loo together.
3. Add up all the house numbers from the school to the corner of Palace Road and Hillside.
4. Estimate the height of the first silver birch in Hillside Park.
5. Draw a bird's eye view of the picnic bench.
6. Estimate the area of the tarmac ball-games area.
7. How much longer is the one o'clock club open in summer than in winter?
8. How many people (maximum) can play tennis in Hillside Park?
9. What shape is tessallated on the wooden back door on the way out of the park?
10. Draw the pattern of shapes on top of the houses on either side of the exit.
11. How many hours is the baker's shop open in one week?
12. What is the fine for not cleaning up dog mess in Palace Road? What if this happens four times?

...

Maths Trail B

1. Count how many poles there are on the way down the slope.
2. Add up the numbers in the phone number on the portable loo.
3. What's the speed limit in Hillside Gardens?
4. What shape is the sundial at 8 Hillside?
5. Estimate the height of the first silver birch tree in Hillside Park.
6. How many people can sit on the benches in the dog-free area?
7. Estimate the area of the tarmac ball-games area.
8. How many uprights are there in the climbing frame?
9. Stand by the playground. Where can you see a cylinder, a cuboid, a large triangle?
10. What age children can go to the one o'clock club?
11. What is the date on the drain by the exit gate?
12. What hours is the baker's shop open?

...

Maths Trail C

1. Count the poles in the railings down the slope.
2. Draw the Fire Hydrant Sign numbers.
3. What shape is the sundial at Hillcroft, 8 Hillside?
4. Count the pink cherry trees.
5. What shapes can you find in the playground? Draw them.
6. How many steps are there between the lawns on the way out?
7. What shapes can you see in the window of Number 23?
8. Draw other patterns that you can see on Number 23.
9. What shape can you see on the speed bumps?
10. What shape is the 'school' sign.
11. How many big yellow letters are on the road outside the school?
12. What is the yellow line pattern on the road?

...

Timetabling

Set a timetable that you are all comfortable with. Give people scope to handle investigations and longer projects within a reasonable length of time. And allow some slack, so that neither children nor teachers feel obliged to perform the miraculous in one day. Decide first about events that involve everyone. Use whole-school gatherings to announce findings, to present children's work and to involve everyone in an activity suitable for all ages. Then share out time for use of the hall, the playground and any other open space. After that the level of detail is up to you. You could allocate time in half-day slots and then leave the rest of the planning to individuals. Or you could opt for a more structured approach. Do whatever suits your school's style.

Remember

scale down rather than up

check that contingencies are covered

make adjustments as you go

check that the resourcing is covered

make it appropriate for your school

check for agreement

30

Outline timetable

	Monday Design and make games	Tuesday Measures
1st session	0930–1020 assemblies (intro Week)	(Y3 calculators)
2nd session	(R calculators)	(Y1 calculators)
3rd session	open-ended activity/ investigation (N/Y4 Maths Trail)	open-ended activity/ investigation (R/Y5 Maths Trail)

Structured timetable

	Monday	Tuesday	Wednesday
8.55 – 9.05	reg	reg	reg
	(15) assembly	(45) Maths in science	
	(60) Maths in picture books – rhymes, jokes, poems Make a book	(30) Maths in the outdoors (maths walk)	Maths in our world (museum trip, with fact sheet and the Three Tasks)
10.20 – 10.40	break	break	
	(45) Maths in art and design	(35) Maths in history	
	(35) Maths in music and drama	(45) Maths in geography	
12.00 – 1.00	lunch	lunch	lunch
1.10	reg	reg	reg
	(35) Maths in cooking	(20) Maths in different languages	(60) Workshop (Friday's presentations)
	(45) Maths in ICT	(60) Workshop (products for maths shop)	(20) Maths on the TV
2.30	break	break	
2.50	(40) Maths in PE	(25) Maths in a story	(20) Maths in history
			(20) Maths in geography
3.30			Maths shop open

Different approaches

One school (see left) went cross-curricular and chose the theme 'Maths in our world'. Another school (see right) focused on shape and space and chose the theme 'Creative mathematics'.

— Cross-curricular
   One of this school's aims is about making connections: between people, between countries and between ideas. Hence the choice of theme. A few sessions picked up on different languages: this is an area where the school wants to enhance the National Curriculum. During the Week, guest speakers visited; there was a trip to a museum; the children ran a maths shop; and there was a final assembly and presentation to families.

— Focus on shape and space
   This school is enthusiastic about the Arts and believes that encouraging children to be creative will help them think creatively in any subject area. The timetable enabled different Year groups to work together and reserved part of the Week for normal school activities. During the Week, a guest artist assisted with art workshops, the children held Structure Parades and they put together a local exhibition.

Outline timetable

	Wednesday		Thursday	Friday		
8.50						
9.00	Normal timetable Y3/Y4. Y5/Y6	Visit to art gallery and sculpture park Nursery/Reception, Y1/Y2	Whole school normal timetable	Normal timetable Y3/Y4, Y5/Y6	Structure parade Nursery/Reception, Y1/Y2	60 mins
10.00				Normal timetable Nursery/Reception, Y1/Y2	Structure parade Y3/Y4, Y5/Y6	60 mins
11.00	break		break	break		
11.15	Normal timetable Y3/Y4, Y5/Y6		Art workshops Nursery/Reception, Y1/Y2, Y3/Y4, Y5/Y6	Whole school normal timetable		60 mins
12.15	lunch		lunch	lunch		
13.15	quiet time		quiet time	quiet time		
13.25	Normal timetable Nursery/Reception, Y1/Y2	Art activities Y3/Y4, Y5/Y6	Art workshops Nursery/Reception, Y1/Y2, Y3/Y4, Y5/Y6	Prepare exhibition, 'sell' tickets on the door		50 mins
14.15				Exhibition (private view) and extraordinary structure parade, relatives invited		50 mins
15.05			60 mins			
15.20	class assembly (Y2:red class)		year group assembly (Y6)	whole school assembly (exhibition moves to local library for two weeks)		

Communicating

Clear, regular communication will help to guarantee the success of your Maths Week. Keep everyone informed, parents as well. When you first tell the children, encourage them to think of ways in which their families or other people in the community could help. The Maths Week can give parents a chance to see what their children are doing in school and to check how they can support them at home. There is potential here for real dialogue: an open session, for example, can dispel the insecurities that some parents have about maths – or shift certain fixed ideas on how it should be taught. Enlist the children's help in organising some events and remember to confirm all arrangements with the teaching assistants, parent helpers and any guests.

Communicate through

updates on the staff noticeboard

staff meetings

the school newsletter

letters to parents

posters

daily bulletins

Maths in Art and Music
4 – 8 July

Our Maths Week is just a month away!
Volunteers needed for:

art workshops (tell the office or Miss Nguru)	music workshops (tell the office or Mr Jamieson)
Year 1 Monday am	Year 6 Monday am
Year 2 Monday pm	Year 5 Monday pm
Year 3 Tuesday am	Year 4 Tuesday am
Year 4 Tuesday pm	Year 3 Tuesday pm
Year 5 Wednesday am	Year 2 Wednesday am
Year 6 Wednesday pm	Year 1 Wednesday pm

Dates for the diary!

OPEN EVENING
Thursday 7 July 6 – 8 pm

ART EXHIBITION AND CONCERT
Friday 8 July 2 – 3.30 pm

Maths Week bulletin
Jan 30th

The artist (Maeve Bryson) has been booked and will talk to Y3/4 on 11 March in the hall at 2 pm.

The group is still looking for helpers to price items for the maths shop.

Please see your almost final timetables (in pigeonholes and on noticeboard).

The group has organised additional funds for café (£100 from Mr Bakhal) plus promise of plates of sweetmeats.

Y5 will definitely do the plant survey with the Horticultural Trust on 12 March.

Maths Week!
Daily Bulletin
Wed 10 March

Year 1 and Year 2	Year 3 and Year 4	Year 5 and Year 6
Outing to Eureka! coach leaves 9.15 am coach returns 3.30 pm	investigation am (insects) swimming survey pm	Maths Trail am DT workshop pm

NB Recipes needed for Friday

School Newsletter

The plans for our Maths Week are going well. The theme is **Fun with Numbers,** and it all starts on Monday 11 November.

We want it to be a very special occasion with lots of exciting events for the children to join in. We shall not follow the normal timetable for the week. Instead we shall have workshops, visits, special assemblies and events and much more.

We shall soon be asking for your support and practical help to:

• run a workshop

• help supervise groups of children

• go with children on outings.

There will be a Maths Fair on Thursday 14 November (starting at 2 pm), which you will all be invited to. We'll send out more details later, but this is just to let you know that it's happening. Come along and see for yourself what the children have been up to. You can try your hand at the latest computer programs, have a go at a maths puzzle or enjoy playing a maths game – after you have followed the maths trail, of course.

The following week we shall display the children's work (opposite the school office) for you all to see if you can call in.

Dear parent

Our Maths Week starts on Monday 11 November, and we need your support. Could you help a teacher with any of these?
– running a workshop
– looking after groups of children
– going with children on outings

We are also looking for people who use maths at work, or in leisure time. Would you share your expertise with some of our children and give them a talk about how maths is involved in what you do? We can discuss it with you first, if you like, to see how we can support you.

If you can help in any way, please return the slip below to your child's teacher. If you can't, don't worry: there are always other times.

Thank you

Marion Elliott
Headteacher

- - - - - - - - - - - - - - - -

I am willing to help with
☐ running a workshop
☐ looking after a group of children
☐ going with children on an outing
☐ giving a talk about how I use maths

I can offer time on Mon/Tues/Wed/Thurs (please circle)

name (please print) . . . .
contact number or email address . . . .

Taking stock

Evaluating the Week

Hold an evaluation session as close to the end of the Week as possible, and involve all the staff. Bring to the meeting evidence if you have it of responses from the children and also feedback from parents or other adults involved. In the meeting, cover the aims and success criteria set out at the beginning, identify the strengths of the Maths Week and any problem areas, and note down any action points for another Maths Week or similar event. Enjoy the moment when you congratulate everyone on their successes and their hard work.

Think about

what you would do as before

what you would do differently

what you would not do again (ever)

whether you have thanked people

Defining success

One school started their evaluation session by forming groups and noting the strengths and weaknesses of the Week on Post-It notes, to be displayed and assessed during the session.

Strengths
Class 4 say they want to be maths teachers

Lots of people from the community contributed

Strengths
Class 5 and 6 organised Maths shop all by themselves

My children love maths now

Weaknesses
Parents' evening clashed with the football match

Too many things planned — not enough time

Weaknesses
Timetable didn't work

Maths and magic presentation too adult, went over kids' heads

Strengths
Maths quilt was a brilliant way of looking at 2D shape

I enjoyed maths week and cooking and i liked the maths week. I enjoyed maths in sport In maths week we planted seeds and we did science on the seeds for what they looked like and how they changed evry day and we did a Dragon in a house for a story called ther as a Dragon fro

I enjoyed Maths We did lots of fu I liked doing the trail. I loved cou many panes of gla the chapel window were 112. I loved my Snail, It Was I liked doing th as Well.

Lots of love Sophie xxxxxx

I have enjoyed Maths week because it has been fun I liked the matise the best thing Was cooking and making a book and doing colouring Maths trail and weighing and going on the computer
Alex

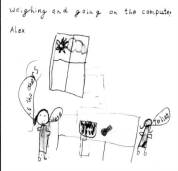

Evaluation check-list

Aims

Which of the intended aims did we achieve, and how well? Were there other aims that we achieved incidentally? Did we meet our success criteria?

Feedback

What informal feedback can people report? How did the children respond?

People

How well did the various collaborations work?

Timetable

Did the organisation work? Was there enough time? Too much?

Budget

Was the money enough? Was it well spent?

Special events

Which visitor would people like to ask again? What outings worked well? Why?

Learning

How would you summarise what the children learned during the Week? What did you learn?

Pleasure

Was it all tremendous fun – or were some bits just not worth the effort?

Strengths and weaknesses

Review the strengths and weaknesses.

Follow-up

What follow-up can be planned for individual classes or groups?

Planning ahead

What is a suitable interval before the next Maths Week? What changes would you recommend? Do you have any new ideas?

Recognising success

One school chose 'Maths and the Environment' as its theme. The long-term project for the whole school was to design and build a maze for a piece of nearby wasteland. At the end of the Maths Week, the teachers assessed whether they had succeeded in their aims, and wrote a report for the headteacher and governors.

— **Aim: to develop thinking skills**
Success criteria:
All children according to their ability were involved in some stages of the planning and decision-making process. They generated ideas and drew plans. They investigated the suitability of different materials and plants and explored the properties of different path materials. They reflected on the purpose of the maze and related it to its location.

— **Aim: to inspire fresh learning**
Success criteria:
All children used pattern or simple algebra to explore and develop maze designs. Very young children used linking cubes and Plasticine; older children developed designs on squared paper, and considered the idea of enlargement. Some of the children in Year 5 and Year 6 used triangulation to draw the original area to scale.

— **Aim: to work in new environment**
Success criteria:
Children explored the wasteland, and drew maps and plans of the area. They visited a local maze and took photographs with a digital camera. Older children explored mazes on the Internet. When the maze was built, some children helped, planting lavender bushes and spreading chipped bark mulch.

— **Aim: to involve members of the community**
Success criteria:
The school had contacted the town council earlier about fast-track approval of plans for the site. A local environmental artist advised the school beforehand and visited the school during the Week to talk and work with children. Parents (including a landscape gardener) helped with the construction of the maze. The maze will be available to all passers-by, and will be maintained by the school and the PTA.

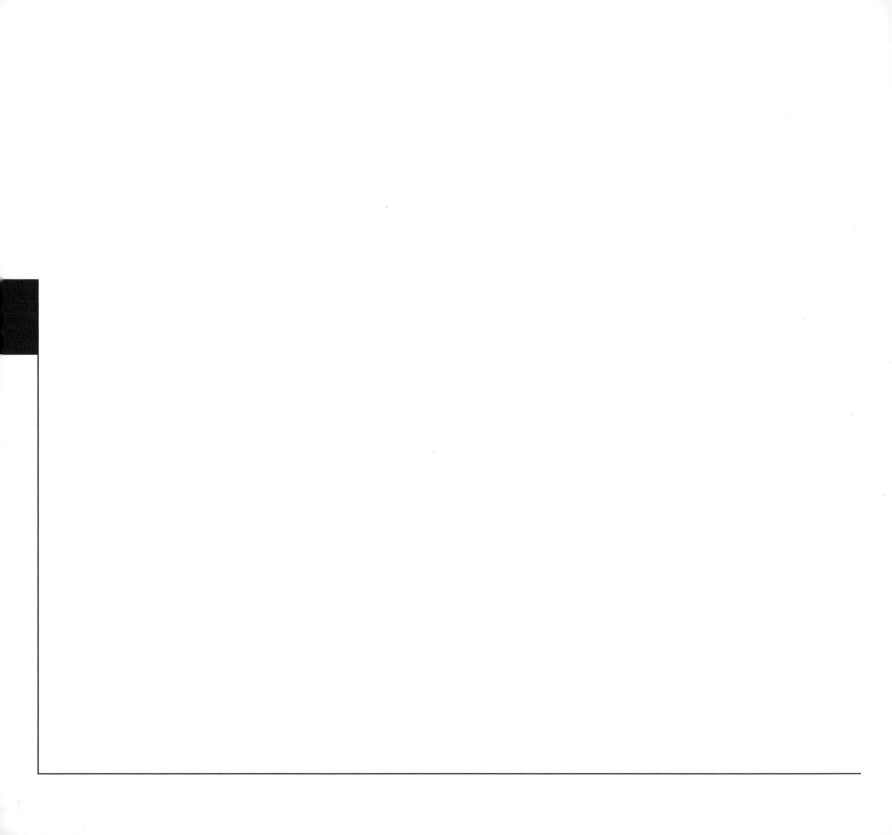

A to Z of ideas

37

Architecture
Art and design
Assemblies
Body measures
Books
Café
Calculators
Calendar
Cards
Chess
Chinese mathematics
Citizenship
Clay
Competitions
Construction
Cooking
Counting systems
Design and technology
Diary
Dice
Dominoes
Drama
Egyptian mathematics

English
Environment
Family
Festivals
Food
Fractions
Games
Gardening
Geoboards
Geography
Giant grids
Greek mathematics
Halves
Hats
History
Home
ICT
Infinity
Investigations
Jokes
Journeys
Juggling
Jumping
Kaleidoscope
Kites

Languages
Library
Logic
Magazine
Magic
Magic squares
Mancala
Maps
Mazes
Mirrors
Money
Music
Needlework
Negative numbers
Nets
Number lines and tracks
Origami
Outings
Patterns
Pets
Physical maths
Playground
Poems
Position

Problems and puzzles
Quiet time
Quilts
Quiz
Reflection
Remainders
Right angles
Rotation
Rotational symmetry
Rubbish
School
Science
Shapes
Shop
Size
Spirals
Sport
Squares
Surveys
Symmetry
Tangrams
Television
Tessellation
Time

Toys
Trails
Transport
Trees
Universe
Unknown
Up
Vedic mathematics
Vegetables
Vertical
Victorians
Vikings
Visitors
Volume
Walks
Water
Weather
Weaving
Weighing
Woodwork
X-axis
X-rays
You
Zeno's paradox
Zero

Architecture

see also: Construction, Design and technology, Environment, Size, Outings, Quilts

Architecture fits well into an historical theme or a design and technology theme, and can form an interesting part of a Maths Walk.

Take an Architecture Walk. Identify several different styles of architecture and discuss the differences by comparing features. For example, compare window sizes and proportions, the number of panes of glass and the size of the panes. Is there stained glass? Does the window surround have any decoration? Collect data and check your findings against resource packs, books and the Internet.

Sketch examples of shapes of windows (or doors or door furniture or roofs or drainpipes…). Look for patterns of brickwork (or wrought iron fencing or decorative features). Use a reference activity sheet to help identify shapes and patterns to look for.

Draw a building, noting size and shape of doors, windows and other features. Decide what rooms it contains, and what evidence there is from the outside of what the inside looks like.

Compare architectural styles in two historical periods or compare an old building with a new one. Look at dates, shapes and patterns. If you can, talk to people who were involved with the construction.

Get hold of an aerial photograph of your school and its surroundings. Find out whether the school buildings or the playground take up the largest area.

Compare an aerial photograph of your school with a map of the same area. Identify the buildings on the photograph. Look at older maps of the same area. See which buildings are still there. On your Walk, see if you can notice what makes some buildings look older than others.

Design your ideal home (a flat, a house, a boat, a caravan, a tree-house, a tent…). Think about the different rooms in your home, their size and layout and shape. Draw elevations of your home, and plans of each floor.

Make prints and patterns, using different objects, to represent part of a building: windows, tiles on the roof, paving on paths. Focus on brickwork and tiling patterns.

Invite an architect in, to describe what it is they do and where mathematics is involved. Find out how they solve problems about where to put water pipes, electricity wires and drains.

Do a survey of your school playground. Find out what people like and don't like. Design a new playground, with play equipment. Design each piece of equipment carefully for size, shape and safety.

Draw a plan of the school showing a route from one place to another. Draw in all the exits. Make a map of the school for visitors, describing how to get to the reception area.

Photograph different styles of building or different features (doors, windows and so on). Use the photos to make a book on your community, or to illustrate a map of the local environment or a maths board game.

Measure the school and make a model one tenth its size. Consider what shape the school would be if you unfolded it. Would it fit inside the playground?

Draw a plan of the school showing where the radiators are. Find out what heats the radiators, and where the boiler is.

Art and design

see also: Architecture, Calendar, Clay, Construction, Design and technology, Kites, Magazine, Needlework, Nets, Origami, Outings, Patterns, Shapes, Size, Tessellations

Art and design activities enliven a Maths Week. This is an opportunity to bring out the strong links between maths and art, and to spend long periods of time on one activity.

Choose a print of a famous painting. Overlay a grid on the painting and make a copy of it on your own grid. Or make a larger version of the painting on a larger grid.

Visit an art gallery and look for themes, such as the use of shapes, of perspective and of repeated pattern.

Tessellate tiles to produce a 3D effect. Dissect a rectangle and slide and stick the cut-off pieces to make a new tessellating tile. Take inspiration from Escher tiling patterns and from Islamic art.

Print patterns using vegetables, sponges, rubber stamps, carbon paper, lino cuts... Make translating, reflecting and rotating patterns. Create reflected and rotational symmetry. Explore shapes made with overlapped printing. Make alphabet prints so that they come out the right way round.

Make a sea serpent in the hall and measure its length and width.

Build a giant in the hall. Or, make a model of the giant's shoe and work out the dimensions of the rest of the giant from the shoe.

Design collages using 2D shapes. Make different shapes with the overlaps. Decide how to fit the shapes together. Make a collage of circles, ovals and curves on round paper. Make a triangle collage on a triangular piece of paper. Include 3D shapes. Make a 3D collage on a box. Make a collage using cylinders.

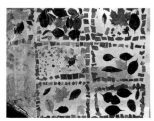

Make a half-size model of yourself. Make clothes for your model. Make your entire family one tenth of their size, and create a room to put them in. Make a pair of shoes for a pixie. Choose a toy car; make a model car twice as big.

Investigate the golden section in the work of different artists (like da Vinci or Mondrian). Look them up on the Internet.

Create small-scale and large-scale drawings and paintings. Make miniature portraits and pictures using magnifying glasses and very fine brushes.

Be Georges Seurat and paint using small dots. Be a Maori artist and use spots. Be Bridget Riley and use dazzling lines.

Make huge mural paintings with paper the size of hoardings. Use charcoal, decorating brushes and thick markers. Make sculptures using florists' wire and tissue paper.

Use computer software to generate designs. Make a display of computer art. Use computers for tiling, for cutting and pasting repeat designs, for reflecting and rotating designs, for making 2D representations of 3D shapes.

Invite an artist to be 'artist-in-residence'.

Assemblies

see also: Drama, Hats, School

Use times when the whole school is gathered together to announce findings from investigations, to present work, and to involve all the children in an activity.

A tessellation assembly: groups of children make large tessellating shapes to show the rest of the school before combining them into one large shape.

A magic calculator assembly: children (and teachers?) enact a scene where a child keys in four digits on a new calculator, only to find they have formed a date in history, and the child goes back in time to a mathematics lesson on that date.

An assembly looking back in time: children from different Year groups present an account of the number system in different periods in history.

A body maths assembly: each child holds a large number on the chest and joins up with the next biggest, and then the person who is 2 bigger, 3 bigger, and so on. Then do some addition or subtraction work with them.

An assembly using an **OHP calculator:** children join in a counting chant as soon as they can see the patterns. Vary the size of the jumps so all ages are involved. Count in 1s, 10s, 100s, 5s, 50s, 3s, backwards and forwards.

B

Body measures

see also: Egyptian mathematics, Size, You

Children enjoy the chance to measure themselves. Watch out for sensitivities about size or shape.

Find out about the history of measures and how many of them relate to body measures: the foot, the inch (a thumb width), the yard (the distance from nose to tip of outstretched arm), the cubit (the length of the forearm).

Devise a measuring system based on body measures. Compare different systems (footwidths, thumbnails, ear lengths…) and see how they differ. Work out the relationship between body measures: is everyone's handspan eleven of their thumbwidths?

Investigate the relationship between body measures. Is three times round your wrist the same as once round your neck? Is your height the same as your reach?

Investigate correlations. Is the person with the longest foot the tallest? Does the person with the longest legs run fastest? Does the person with the longest finger have the longest toe? Present the findings in graphs and charts.

Find the mode, median and mean of foot sizes in one year group.

Measure both feet. Are both feet the same size? Make a bar chart of number of children and length of left feet, and another chart of right feet. Are they the same?

Draw round your foot and then your shoe. Does your shoe fit properly? What does this tell you about shoes?

Use displacement to find out the volume of your fist.

Books

see also: Calendar, Design and technology, Diary, English, Library, Visitors

You can probe the mathematics of how books are constructed and the way they work. You can also use story books to investigate mathematical themes. But do this sensitively, without spoiling the magic of the story.

Pick a book and find what letter appears most often in it. Is it a different letter in each book? What about a book written in Turkish? How does this help you play hangman, or decipher simple codes?

Find out why printers like to print books with multiples of 16 pages, and

how they lay the pages out when they make a printers' plate. If possible, visit a printing press to see how books are printed.

Explore the patterns of page numbering. What do you notice about the page numbers on the left and the page numbers on the right? Is this the same in all books? What about newspapers?

Use books on mirrors, dominoes, games and puzzles to encourage problem-solving skills and lateral thinking.

Read stories such as *Alice in Wonderland* (Lewis Carroll), *The Phantom Tollbooth* (Norton Juster), *Where the Wild Things are* (Maurice Sendak), *The Ship that Flew* (Hilda Lewis) or *The Magic Faraway Tree* (Enid Blyton), and set up problems for children to solve related to the themes in the book. Make a pulley for the basket for *The Lighthouse Keeper's Lunch* (Ronda and David Armitage). Make a Flat Stanley from their own outline that can be posted

in through a letter box (*Flat Stanley*, Jeff Brown). Use the giant theme in *Jim and the Beanstalk* (Raymond Briggs) for the whole of the maths week.

Explore ways of finding the thickness of a page in a book. Find which book has the thinnest or the thickest pages. Find out which books of the same size are the heaviest, and why.

Make books: make a book on big numbers, or on the 2 times table, or on how to make the 16 times table, or on things that come in pairs or in fives. Make a maze puzzle book.

Give children in Years 5 and 6 a project: to make a number book for children in Nursery and Reception.

Set up a second-hand bookshop and sell books children have made or books brought in from home. Vote on how to spend the proceeds.

Buy in some mathematics books to sell on to parents.

C

Café

see also: Cooking, Food, Outings, Shop, Vegetables, Visitors

Running a café, whether real or pretend, involves

many different aspects of mathematics, from costing a menu to designing patterned tablecloths and weighing out ingredients. This can be a financial competence project for a Year 5 or Year 6 class, or a mini-project for Reception in the role play area.

Mathematical activities associated with setting up and running a café include estimating and weighing quantities, doubling quantities, measuring capacity, timing, using shaped cutters to create different shapes, planning the layout of tables and chairs, pricing and producing a menu, painting or printing patterns for table mats and tablecloths, making out bills and giving change.

Book the hall for one class to turn it into a café, which children, parents and teachers can visit at the end of the school day. Involve the children in keeping track of the money and recording the finances of the café.

Serve food from a variety of cultures at an open event, with the help of teachers and parents.

Design a menu that gives the cost of each item in three currencies.

Prepare and serve pretend food: ribbons of paper for noodles, to be eaten with chopsticks; rice, dried beans and pulses for curries and stir-fries; play-dough shaped to form triangular samosas or circular pizzas.

Calculators

see also: **Problems and puzzles, Remainders**

Use calculator activities to encourage number recognition, estimating and checking.

Set a new calculator challenge for the whole school each day, using ones that can be tackled at different levels, such as 'Write in words the biggest number that you can get on your calculator', or 'Work out and show on the calculator how old you are in years or months or days

or hours or minutes or seconds'. Present these as a whole school, or individually in the classrooms.

Give children practice in estimating. Write calculations on cards and put a multiple of 10 below the sum.

44 + 15	51 − 8	19 × 13	12 × 61
60	40	300	700

Shuffle the cards and put them face down on the table. Player One turns over the top card, looks at the sum and says aloud whether the number underneath is more or less than the answer. Player Two checks the answer on the calculator. If Player One was correct, they keep the card; if not, it goes to the bottom of the pile. Player Two takes the top card from the pile and play continues.

Aim for zero (working in pairs). Player One chooses a six-digit number and puts it in their partner's calculator. Player Two has

to reduce that number to zero in no more than four moves. They take it in turns until each child has had three (or five) turns.

Ask children to make the calculator show 30: they can press any five keys but must press five keys exactly. Then try with the same rules and a new target number.

Sell calculators, together with books of games and activities, in a maths shop run by the children. Hold a workshop for parents on calculators, with intriguing puzzles and games.

Investigate large numbers or numbers with a great many decimals. Have you lived more or less than a million minutes? What is the largest number you can show in your calculator display (and the smallest)?

Explore number patterns:

1 × 3, 11 × 33, 111 × 333; and 1 × 6 + 1, 12 × 6 + 2, 123 × 6 + 3.

Study square numbers. What number was multiplied by itself to give these answers?

9　25　100　4　400
9801　10000　1·44?

Calendar

see also: **Art and design, Festivals, Time**

You could make a calendar from the Maths Week, celebrating the children's achievements, and either sell it or give it away.

Make a calendar for the year, decorating each month with children's own artwork (exploring shape, size and pattern) or a maths puzzle.

Produce a calendar for next term. Draw up the grid of days and weeks using squared paper, and decorate it with tessellations or other repeating patterns.

Draw a large poster showing all the days of the year and display it in a public area so children can mark on it their birthday. Are there any days with two birthdays? Or three?

Choose a particular month or season and make a class calendar, with a column for a daily mathematical problem.

Find out about famous mathematicians – and about ideas based on a mathematical view of the world – and then make a calendar that describes each of twelve ideas.

Use the computer to print out a simple calendar for every child in the class. Decide whether each child can choose a theme or whether to allocate one. Or just use it to note important dates or to inscribe a daily maths problem invented by individual children.

Investigate the mathematics of calendars: how to work out the day of the week a person was born from their birth date; the pattern of leap years; the pattern of sevens in the dates of each month.

Investigate lunar and solar calendars. Research the history of the Julian calendar and the Gregorian calendar. Compare this with the Chinese calendar. Find out about leap years, and about other solutions to the problem of adjusting the calendar, such as inserting a thirteenth month every few years. How is the timing of Easter, Ramadan or the Chinese Spring Festival calculated?

Design a calendar that reinforces the cross-curricular shape of the Week. Embed mathematical content in the form of puzzles, questions, games or facts. Give each season a theme.

Cards

see also: Games, Number lines and tracks, Physical maths

Many mathematical skills can be practised in cards activities, using either playing cards or number cards. Card games often require strategic thinking and fast mental calculation.

Be aware that some families are not happy for their children to use playing cards.

Ask the whole class to make a pack of giant playing cards from sheets of A5 card. Use them for simple addition activities, for sorting, for symmetry work, and for individual or group games.

Play 'Guess the card'. Spread the cards out face up. One child writes down the name of a card (such as Queen of hearts or 5 ♠) and the others have to identify the card with as few questions as possible. Only yes/no answers are allowed.

Play 'Tens'. This is a game for two to four players. The ace is 1, Jack is 11, Queen is 12 and King is 13. Shuffle the cards and deal five to each player. Players look at their cards and take turns to put down a card in the middle of the table. Whenever a player's card makes the total of the cards in the middle add up

to 10 or a multiple of 10, that player wins those cards and puts them face down near them. The game is over when all cards are played; the winner is the player with most cards.

Play 'Patience'. Individual children can play this, or a pair can work together. The ace is 1, Jack is 11, Queen is 12 and King is 13. Shuffle the pack and lay out the top twelve cards face up:

Cover any two cards that add to 14 with another two cards (face up). Do this until you use up all the cards. If you get stuck, reshuffle all the cards and start again. Variation: use cards Ace to 10 and aim for 11; use cards Ace to Jack and aim for 12; use a 3 × 3 array instead of 4 × 3; cover two or three cards that add to your total.

Play 'Addsnap' in pairs, with 0–9 number cards. Use two of each card. Share the cards out between the players. Players each put down a

card at the same time. The first to add them and call the answer keeps those cards. The player with the most cards wins.

Optional: another child is arbitrator; they use a calculator to check.

Variations: Takesnap, where players call the difference; Multisnap, where players call the product; Divisnap, where players call the remainder (which may be zero) after dividing the larger number by the smaller.

Play 'Avoid 10' in pairs or groups of three, with 1–9 number cards. You need two of each card. Shuffle the cards and deal five to each player. Take turns to choose a card to put on the table, face up. The loser is the first player to put down a card which makes 10 – or a multiple of 10 – when added to any other of the cards on the table.

If you play a 2 you 'll lose, because 8 and 2 is 10.

| 9 | 7 | 9 | 6 |

If you play a 5 you 'll lose, because 5 plus 9 plus 6 equals 20.

Play 'Frustration' in pairs, with 0–9 number cards. Spread the cards face up on the table. Players take turns to pick a card from the table. The first player to collect two or more cards whose numbers add up to 15 wins. Play five games to decide the overall winner.

Take three number cards and arrange them into all possible three-digit numbers; record them, starting with the smallest. Now try four cards.

Chess

see also: Games

Chess involves logical, strategic thinking, and a sense of 2D position and movement, skills that children can transfer to mathematical problem solving.

Set up a chess club. Invite Year 6 children to help, and ask interested parents.

Hold a chess championship within the class or school.

Make or buy a giant chess set for the school hall or playground.

Include chess problems in a school magazine, or in a problem-of-the-day display. Discuss possible solutions.

Give children a chessboard and sets of play figures, such as dinosaurs or space characters, and ask them to make up a game of strategy where different characters have different moves. They play, trial, improve, then record the rules to their game for others to play.

Ask for solutions to mathematical problems about chess moves or the chess board. If you write 1 on the first square, 2 on the next, 3 on the next, and so on, and then add up the numbers, what will the total be? If a knight starts here, can he get to any square on the board by making a 'knight's move'?

Chinese mathematics

see also: Counting systems, Egyptian mathematics, Greek mathematics, Tangrams

Describe the Pythagoras theorem. Explain how a Chinese mathematician worked this out 1,000 years before Pythagoras.

Look at a 100-grid written in Chinese. Work out the correspondence between the Chinese numbers and international numbers.

零	一	二	三	四	五	六	七	八	九
十	十一	十二	十三	十四	十五	十六	十七	十八	十九
二十	二十一	二十二	二十三	二十四	二十五	二十六	二十七	二十八	二十九
三十	三十一	三十二	三十三	三十四	三十五	三十六	三十七	三十八	三十九
四十	四十一	四十二	四十三	四十四	四十五	四十六	四十七	四十八	四十九
五十	五十一	五十二	五十三	五十四	五十五	五十六	五十七	五十八	五十九
六十	六十一	六十二	六十三	六十四	六十五	六十六	六十七	六十八	六十九
七十	七十一	七十二	七十三	七十四	七十五	七十六	七十七	七十八	七十九
八十	八十一	八十二	八十三	八十四	八十五	八十六	八十七	八十八	八十九
九十	九十一	九十二	九十三	九十四	九十五	九十六	九十七	九十八	九十九

Cut a Chinese 100-grid up to make a jigsaw, and invite children to use the pattern of numbers to put it together again.

Find out about the Chinese abacus. Hold a competition between someone using the abacus to work out a calculation, and someone using the calculator.

Experiment with the old Chinese method of finding square roots. Starting with 1, subtract the odd numbers (in sequence) from the square number, until you get zero. Count up the number of steps and you have the square root.

25 is the square number

$25 - 1 = 24$	step 1
$24 - 3 = 21$	step 2
$21 - 5 = 16$	step 3
$16 - 7 = 9$	step 4
$9 - 9 = 0$	step 5

Five steps: so the square root of 25 is 5.

Citizenship

see also: Drama, Money

Some topics covered in the Maths Week will address citizenship as well as mathematics. Both areas draw on problem-solving skills and creative thinking.

Debate topics such as the value of money in our society, or how we decide what something is worth or how we measure the difference an individual can make.

Bring in articles in the press (including charts if possible) that report changes in, for example, climate patterns, children's eating habits, or the wages of nurses or social workers.

Analyse the data and the way in which it is presented. Is it clear? Discuss the implications of the data for the individuals concerned, and for society.

Look at what a family needs to spend money on, and what they might want to spend it on. Look at household bills and work out how much the electricity or gas or telephone and so on cost a week.

Discuss the value of different school rules. Choose one rule and hold a class vote on whether it should stay. Present the results in a chart and agree whether (and how) to propose any real changes.

Clay

see also: Art and design

Make your Maths Week memorable by inviting a potter to hold a clay workshop.

Teach techniques for building pots, like rolling out slabs and building them into a three-dimensional form; or making coils by rolling the clay into strips, forming these into a spiral to make a base and building up the sides by laying more coils around the edge of the base, one on top of another.

Decorate pots by adding smaller cut-out clay shapes or creating surface texture or pattern by impressing objects, or by roughening the surface with a variety of tools. Compare patterns and techniques.

Investigate the time it takes to fire a pot in a kiln. Discuss the temperatures, and compare these with a domestic oven.

Compare the capacity of pots: does a tall thin pot contain more or less than a short squat pot? Make three different shaped jugs, each with the capacity to hold half a pint of milk.

Make play food for the shop in Reception.

Competitions

see also: Dice, Dominoes, Games, Hats, Jokes

Some children feel excluded by competitions. Invent ones where all children win in one way or another, or where the competition is a game and not about competence. If you have a visitor at the time when judging is required, invite them to judge and give the awards.

Invent a maths game. A child in Year 4 came up with a weighing game, where two players have ten minutes to find things that weigh more than 100 g and less than 200 g; the player who finds most items wins. A child in Year 6 devised a game involving adding numbers and writing the answers only, then swapping work and working out the other player's starting numbers.

Hold a fancy dress competition – making and wearing mathematical hats, for example, or aprons.

Guess the weight of a bag of rice or the number of sweets, pebbles or conkers in a jar.

Design and make a counting book suitable for a four-year-old. Award prizes or certificates to the team who make the funniest or most inventive or most unusual one.

Construction

see also: Architecture, Art and design, Design and technology, Home, Physical maths, Size, Woodwork

Construction activities offer opportunities for collaboration, give practice in problem solving and link with other areas of the curriculum.

Make a self-supporting bridge out of one sheet of newspaper. Who has made the strongest bridge?

Make a tall tower using linking cubes. Work out its statistics: number of cubes, height and weight.

Combine all the towers to make a city of skyscrapers. Use a camera to record what this looks like from above and from various angles.

Create a tower using 3D shapes or old boxes, where each shape is different from the one before.

Use rolled-up cylinders of newspaper and make the tallest tower you can using triangular structures.

Make models from Lego, building blocks or from old boxes. Make the school, the Houses of Parliament, a space station or a tall and leaning Tower of Pisa.

Make models from different 3D shapes. Create a tall structure using different shapes, where each shape has to be different from the one before. Make something lifesize, using large computer boxes or shoe boxes.

Cooking

see also: Café, Food, Vegetables

If you have enough adult support, everyone can have a go at some cooking. Health and safety requires that cooking is an adult-directed activity, but children can still have control of parts of the process. Make sure that the adults know what has to be left to the children to decide. Children can help by choosing recipes, writing shopping lists, doing the shopping, planning the cooking session, and sharing out the food when it is ready. They can measure and weigh out the ingredients themselves. This includes learning how to chop, stir, mix, beat, whisk, sift and strain things themselves – and practise separating eggs.

Make banana smoothies. For two people, blend one banana, 50 ml orange juice, 50 ml pineapple juice, and two ice cubes. What ingredients will you need for four people, or ten people, or 30 people?

Weigh and sort different dried fruits, nuts and

cereals. Design a breakfast muesli dish. Work out the proportions of each ingredient.

Prepare and serve food for a breakfast cafe: tea, milk, orange juice, toast, cereal.

Make Chapatis

500 gm wholewheat flour

150 ml warm water

10 ml vegetable oil

pinch of salt

Instructions: Add the water, oil and salt to the flour. Mix with a fork, and then with your hands. Knead the dough for about 10 minutes. Cut it into 6 equal chunks. Roll each chunk into a very thin pancake, about 20 cm across. Heat a frying pan or a griddle pan until it is hot. Cook each chapati for about half a minute on each side.

Make a cake from a recipe and weigh it before you cook it. Weigh it again when it is cooked.

Grow some cress. On the day it is ready to pick, make bread with the whole class. Children enjoy kneading bread to make it rise. Put some cream in a screw top jar with a little salt. Children take turns to shake it and turn it into butter. Feast on fresh bread, butter and cress.

Prepare three squash drinks in three different strengths: one with 1 tablespoon of squash, one with 2 tablespoons, and one with 3 tablespoons. Do a tasting survey and find out what type each person likes best.

Follow a recipe. Now work out double, or treble, or half, or a quarter, of the recipe. Cost the ingredients in each case.

Choose something to make to eat that you can also buy in a shop or supermarket. Work out the price for the shop-bought and home-made versions. Work out which is cheaper,

and why. Make a list of the ingredients in each version. Discuss the difference.

Bake breads from around the world for a fund-raising stall run during the Week. Conduct a bread tasting session to find out which is the most popular. Record the information on graphs.

Work in mixed age groups and cook something to take home.

Prepare a picnic lunch for the class: fruit, drinks, sandwiches, cake.

Demonstrate how to make a favourite dish.

Counting systems

see also: Chinese mathematics, Egyptian mathematics, Greek mathematics, Vedic mathematics

Compare Egyptian and Greek counting systems.

Compare Chinese and Hindi counting systems.

Investigate the finger counting methods of different cultures, such as the Masai finger counting system or the finger signs of native Americans.

Investigate the Yoruba number system.

Write up your findings for the school magazine.

D

Design and technology

see also: Architecture, Art and design, Construction, Egyptian mathematics, Gardening, History, Home, ICT, Kaleidoscope, Kites, Magazine, Size, Symmetry, Water, Woodwork

Design and technology projects enable children to

use problem-solving skills in a real environment, to work with 2D or 3D shapes and investigate position and movement, and to create something tangible.

Design a window box, a school bag or school crest, a building, or a clock.

Read Anne Fine's *Design a Pram* with the children.

Design a house for your favourite toy using large construction materials and junk boxes.

Draw a room of your own design, to scale. Now make a model of it.

Design and print wallpaper for a doll's house, dungeon or castle.

Make a timer that can measure a minute, using materials and tools from a selection on display.

Design and make the highest structure you can using just newspaper and tape – or art straws and tape. What is its height?

Make tetrahedrons.

Hold a workshop to design a Viking long ship, pyramid or Greek temple.

Investigate different tools and how they work.

Diary

see also: Magazine

Keeping a diary of the Week encourages children to reflect on their learning and their achievements. Include drawings, puzzles and stories.

Write up individual maths diaries. Set aside time each day for this.

Create a class diary of the Week that can be shared with other children or parents (by reading parts aloud in an assembly or displaying it at an open day or by the children taking a copy home at some point following the Week).

Dice

see also: Games

Children play an active role in generating random numbers every time they use dice to get numbers for their calculations. Dice promote calculation skills, number recognition and an understanding of factors and number properties. Older children can use them in discussion about chance and probability.

Roll a dice. Write down the number. Keep doubling it until you get past 50. Show the final number to a partner; can they work out your dice number?

Take turns to roll a giant dice. Whoever rolls the dice chooses an action first (patting your head, for example); then, if the number is a 3, all the children in the group pat their heads three times.

Take turns to roll a dice. Collect that number of beans. After three goes

each, line up the beans to see who has the most.

Take turns to roll a dice. Pick up that number of coins. After three turns each, count up your money. Spin a more/less spinner to see whether the person with more or with less money wins.

Roll five 0–9 dice (or roll one dice five times). Write the numbers on a whiteboard. Arrange the numbers to make a two-digit and a three-digit number. Aim to make numbers that will give the smallest remainder when the larger number is divided by the smaller.

Dominoes

see also: Games, Halves

Dominoes are a structured set of materials with their own internal logic, for use in a range of mathematical problem-solving activities and games.

Practise fractions with Year 6 children. Remove all

dominoes with blanks and spread the remainder face down on the table. The children pick up a domino and place it vertically with the lower number at the top; they read the number as a fraction, and simplify the fraction if need be. They record the number on a fraction line in order, from least to greatest.

Give children domino games to take home and play with their families. For example, provide an outline of 'worms', each three dominoes long: children record which three dominoes they want to place in each outline (remembering that the worm must have 24 spots).

Play 'Addition dominoes'. Instead of arranging dominoes so that the ends match, the touching numbers have to add up to 6.

Include dominoes in a lunchtime games club.

Include double-nine and double-twelve sets, and a variety of domino games. Discuss strategies for winning the conventional game of dominoes. Sort all the muddled dominoes into complete sets. (To do this, children have to find out the structure behind a set of dominoes.)

Invent your own sets of logical, domino-like games. Invent new rules. Make up rules for chains of dominoes. Make a set of triangular dominoes that works as a set.

Drama

see also: Books, Citizenship, Television

Dramatise stories with a mathematical content. Read the story aloud first and then improvise a dramatisation. Include issues like money. See *Something Special for Me* (Vera B Williams), *Treehorn's Treasure* (Florence Parry Heide) or *The Bed and Breakfast Star* (Jacqueline Wilson).

d
d

Find out if performing arts troupes, travelling puppeteers, storytellers or entertainers have anything mathematical in their repertoire. There are a surprising number that do.

Invite circus performers to demonstrate juggling and other circus skills. Produce a display that shows the mathematics behind the magic of the circus.

Organise a theatre trip for the end of term. Remember to set a budget, estimate costs and check timing and transport arrangements. (This project will reinforce the financial capability skills of Year 5 children.)

Egyptian mathematics

see also: Body measures, Chinese mathematics, Counting systems, Greek mathematics

As well as exploring the Egyptian contribution to mathematics, you could examine the mathematical implications of other aspects of ancient Egyptian culture (buildings, calendars, trade).

Study the Egyptians' number system, and write some numbers using it. Make a display of the system, and some numbers, and challenge the viewer to work out the value of these numbers – provide the answers hidden under a flap.

1 | 2 || 3 ||| 4 |||| 5 |||||
6 ||||| | 7 ||||| || 8 ||||| ||| 9 ||||| |||| 10 ∩

100 ℛ 1000 ⚘ 10000 ⌐ 100000 ⸼ 1000000 𓀀

Hieroglyphs were written from right to left

eg.: 256 ||||| ∩∩∩∩∩ ℛℛ

Investigate the Egyptians' measures of length, which were often based on the human body. Invent your own body measures and use them to measure a book, table or classroom.

Investigate how the Egyptians dealt with fractions, and the rules they had for writing fractions. They only used unitary fractions (with 1 as the numerator), so five eighths was a challenge.

Learn to do Egyptian multiplication, which involves doubling and halving.

Learn what a pyramid is in mathematics. Make pyramids from card or Clixi. Make the net of a pyramid from paper. Make a giant pyramid big enough to climb inside.

Make stepped pyramids from linking cubes or Lego and investigate the number patterns involved.

English

see also: Books, Diary, Drama, Library, Poems

Reading, writing, speaking and listening are essential to the understanding of mathematics. In a Maths Week children have the opportunity to talk about and debate mathematical ideas, to listen to each other's presentations, to write reports, rules and instructions, and to read word problems.

Read stories with a mathematical content, like *The six blind men and the Elephant* (Clare Turpin) and *The Shopping Basket* (John Burningham). Discuss the mathematical ideas.

Make up stories with a mathematical content to print in the school magazine or to produce as books for the library. Use an idea from another book, such as following a journey round objects, as in *Rosie's Walk* (Pat Hutchins) and *Bears in the Night* (Stan Berenstain); or inventing a flat world, as in *Flatland* (Edwin A Abbott) and *Flat Stanley* (Jeff Brown).

Write a book review of a maths book or book of maths poems. Invent a mathematical poem. Write a haiku with seventeen syllables.

Write a shopping list of food for a party:
one birthday cake
two giant packets of crisps
three tubs of ice cream
four loaves of bread…
Think of a price per item and find the total cost.

Read all or part of *The Number Devil* (Hans Magnus Enzensberger) with Year 5 and 6 children. It tells the story of twelve-year-old Robert, who fears numbers and hates maths. Then, in his dreams, he meets the Number Devil and is introduced to the amazing world of numbers: infinite numbers; prime numbers; numbers that magically appear in triangles; and numbers that expand without end.

Invent a board game and write down the instructions for it.

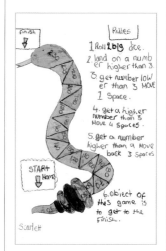

Discuss the idea of a world without numbers. What would this world be like?

Environment

see also: **Architecture, Body measures, Gardening, Rubbish, Science, Trails, Trees, Walks, Weather**

The Maths Week offers time to explore the environment, and gives an opportunity for focused data-handling work.

Focus on... the growing environment.

Hold a maths walk in a nearby park or green area, and collect seeds and leaves to classify. Take photographs of the trees, and make an identification chart of the trees, the leaves and the seeds.

Study the life cycle of an oak tree, from seed to full-grown tree, looking at changes in size, weight and spread. Explore ways of finding out the tree's height.

Invent problems: if it takes six ants three minutes to carry a leaf to their nest, how long would it take 600 ants to dispose of a pile of 3,300 leaves?

Keep a weather book: chart the inches of rainfall over the last month, or look at the shapes and patterns of cirrus, cumulus and nimbus clouds.

Look at how rice is grown; then weigh different amounts and calculate how much you would need to feed a family of seven.

Discuss pollution and the environment; combine this with a trip to a shop or local supermarket; look at packaging and recycling and the quantities involved.

Focus on... the human or social environment.

Collect measurements of yourselves. Explore questions such as: Is twice round your wrist the same as once round your neck? What is the average height of the children in Year 6?

Examine eyesight. How far can babies see at birth, at one month and at six months?

Investigate smell. Do different places have certain smells? Does everything have a smell? What are people's favourite smells?

Are some smells stronger than others? Experiment with sugar, coffee and nails.

Make patterns with fingerprints and note the different shapes. Classify the fingerprints into types.

Focus on... the built environment.

Hold a Maths Trail in the local area. Look at the style of housing; estimate how many people live in three different dwelling places on one road; find out about the local history and how and why changes have happened over time.

Make a map of your journey. Put key locations on the map. Compare the map with an aerial photo.

Go on a maths walk. Look at road signs, street signs and their mathematical content.

Focus on... the school environment.

Walk around the school and its immediate environment, stopping to sketch or photograph designated places.

Do a pedestrian traffic count in one corridor at different times during the day and present the data in a table or graph showing time of day and number of people counted over a set period. Suggest ways to ease congestion.

How many children are there in the whole school? How many teachers or adults are there? What is the ratio of children to teachers or to adults?

Research an agreed environmental topic, using the Internet to access data.

Write a poem that uses numbers and is on the theme of the environment.

Design a postcard to send friends, using mathematical content to make an environmental point.

Family

see also: **Café, Dominoes, Home, Magazine, Pets, Visitors**

If family members are interested and involved in children's mathematics learning, this will motivate children and help them develop a positive attitude to their own learning.

Make a display showing how numbers are written in a range of languages. Use samples provided by parents where possible.

Organise a maths games workshop for all ages, from toddlers to grandparents.

Give children work to take home that will involve other

family members – like games, puzzles, lessons for parents, a maths quiz or a themed maths walk.

Festivals

see also: Calendar, Citizenship

Festivals and celebrations have rituals associated with them that can link well with mathematical explorations. The Maths Week may involve aspects of a festival: cards and invitations, food, parties, decorations, presents, calendars… The Week may also take place at the same time as a festival, which you can weave into your timetable.

For the Chinese Spring Festival (the Chinese New Year), discuss the lunar and solar calendars; explain that the Chinese call the first day of the New Year 'Day One' (*chu yi*), the second 'Day Two' (*chu er*) and so on, up to the fifteenth day (*shi wu*), when the Chinese celebrate the Lantern Festival and the Spring Festival ends.

For the Lantern Festival, design and make Chinese lanterns or fans, and paint numbers or patterns or different shapes on them.

For the Mid-Autumn Festival in China (also known as the Moon Festival), hold a tea party (looking up at the moon) and recite poems on a mathematical theme.

For Christmas, make decorations and explore pattern, symmetry and numbers; investigate time; find out more about astronomy; or draw a map of Mary and Joseph's journey to Bethlehem.

Make paper chains with repeating patterns. Record your instructions for making the pattern. What is the longest paper chain you can make from one sheet of A4 paper?

Make and cut out a five- or six-pointed star. How many different shaped 2D stars can you make? How many different 3D stars can you make?

For Diwali, investigate light. What different kinds of candle are there? Who uses them, and for what purpose? Invent a really safe holder for a candle.

For Easter, hold an Easter parade, where children make mathematical hats; roll painted eggs; make an Easter collage from 1 to 10 (1 Easter rabbit, 2 Easter bonnets, 3 Easter eggs, and so on). Hard boil some eggs and decorate them with symmetrical patterns. Design and make a box to hold an Easter egg where you can see the egg inside.

Investigate and create Rangoli patterns. How are they made up? What are the rules for repeating the pattern?

For Ramadan, work on symmetry and pattern using examples of Islamic art and tiling.

Design and make an invitation card. Make an envelope to go with it. Make a pop-up card, and write instructions for how to make it. Design the card on the computer.

Find the least amount of wrapping paper you need to wrap some prizes.

Wallpaper the outside of a box to hold the prizes.

Make a countdown chart of days until the Maths Week, Pancake Day, Diwali, Easter, the summer holidays… Make a countdown calendar with doors that open and pictures or presents behind.

Design a carnival mask, making sure it has a symmetrical design. Now use your masks as part of a symmetrical dance.

Food

see also: Café, Cooking, Geography, Science, Vegetables, Visitors, Volume, Weighing

Food offers opportunities for planning, problem solving, and data handling.

Work out how to share six sticks of rock fairly between four people – or seven sticks of rock between five people.

Draw a plan of the tables in the dining area and try to think of a better way of arranging them.

Find out how much food is thrown away each day at school. How much is that a week? A year? Are there any alternatives to throwing food away?

Survey all the children in the class to identify their favourite food.

Plan a class party: the menu, drinks, games, timing. Then have the party.

Set up role play areas: a restaurant, or a pizza parlour, or a supermarket, or an internet food delivery service.

Design a nutritious and balanced menu for a main meal. Now design an unhealthy, unbalanced meal. What is the difference in nutrition, in cost, in preparation, in preference…?

Examine your favourite breakfast cereal. How is it packaged? What volume of cereal is contained in the packet? Design and make a packet that holds the same amount but takes up less space.

Investigate ways of cutting a square sandwich in half, or quarters.

Survey the number of pips in apples or oranges. Put the results into a chart and find the mode, median and mean.

Find out what the others in your group had to eat and drink yesterday. Check how many calories they ate. Use a calorie chart. Put the results into a spreadsheet to work it out.

Work out the cost of a day's food. Look at what percentage this is of someone's earnings. What if they were earning the minimum wage? Find out the percentage of income that is spent on food in other countries: Mexico, Bangladesh, Sweden, the USA. Display the findings as graphs or pictograms. Write some general statements about the

results: 'Most people…', 'Only a few people…'.

Investigate bananas. Check where they come from by looking at labels in different shops. Find out how much farmers who grow bananas are paid for them (about 11p a kilogram). Check how much they cost in the supermarket (about £1.20 a kilogram). Look at the economics of this, and search for explanations for the difference in these prices. Design posters to illustrate the facts.

Investigate how food is stacked in a supermarket. What is the best way of saving space and packing the most tins or boxes or bottles in one area?

Find out where the main ingredients come from in tins and packets of food. Investigate the ingredients – they are listed in quantity order. Are there any surprises? Does sugar appear where you wouldn't expect it? What does 'hydrogenated' mean? What percentage of the

product is water? Present the information in graphs, and make statements to interpret the findings.

Fractions

see also: Dominoes, Egyptian mathematics, Halves, Tangrams

Look at a display that shows a fraction of several objects – a section of a plate, half of a scarf, part of a design… . Choose an object and draw the whole of it.

Games

see also: Cards, Chess, Competitions, Dominoes, Family, Journeys, Jumping, Mancala, Mazes, Money, Negative numbers, Rotation, Television

Games give children enjoyment, purpose and a context for practising and exploring mathematical ideas. There is almost no part of maths that cannot be turned into a game. Outdoor and physical games allow young children to learn actively with their whole body.

A Maths Week gives you the chance to set up games workshops.

Set out a game on each table and hold a workshop where, for one hour, children move between tables playing the games.

Play 'Musical numbers'. Each child has a number card. (It doesn't matter if there are duplicate numbers.) The children dance to music; when the music stops, announce a category (such as 'odd numbers', 'numbers over 100', or 'multiples of 5'). Children with these numbers sit down, and the game continues. The players still dancing at the end are the winners.

Play a marathon session of a popular board game.

Make board games using dice and counters: when a player lands on a particular kind of square, they choose from a pack of Challenge cards ('say your 2 times table', 'count up in multiples of 10 from 50 to 210', 'divide 16 by 8 and

move back that number of spaces', 'subtract 290 from 3000'); another child checks their answer with a calculator.

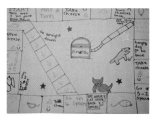

Make board games on a theme such as Treasure Island. Take the original (or a copy) home as a gift for parents. Make a good, laminated copy with proper pieces as a library copy to be borrowed by different classes. Set up a box of invented games for use in wet playtimes.

Invent games that use tracks, boards, dominoes, playing cards, dice or counters. Older children can identify the maths in the game they are inventing and decide what age range it is suitable for. Try out the invented games and modify them to make them even more interesting.

Invent a game to be played on a 0–100 number line.

Set up large-scale counting games outside, such as throwing beanbags in a bucket, or jumping on numbered shapes. Make a maths circuit: jump four times on the mat, go over the stool, through the hoop and between the cones, do three hops… .

Play 'Tables chase', with adult support. Give each child a card with a number in the multiplication tables, made by cutting up a multiplication grid. (It doesn't matter if there are duplicate numbers.) One child is the Chaser – at the blow of a whistle, they run around for thirty seconds catching people who, when caught, sit out on a mat. Whenever there are three children on the mat whose numbers make a multiplication trio – like 2, 4 and 8 (2 × 4 = 8) or 3, 7 and 21 (3 × 7 = 21) – they rejoin the game. Ask an adult to supervise the mat. When the Chaser has had three goes, they choose someone from the mat to take over the role.

Gardening

see also: Environment, Playground, Shop, Weather

A school garden gives you lots of scope for maths work. On a smaller scale, you can use outdoor pots, shrubs and border flowerbeds, and indoors you can plant seeds, bulbs and cuttings. You can grow mushrooms, amaryllis plants, mung beans…

Raise money for a tub garden. Organise a trip to a garden centre or nursery to buy the tubs, compost, plants and anything else. Agree the budget first.

Study a collection of gardening tools and talk about how they work.

Measure the pH factor in selected soil. What do your results tell you? Look in a book of garden plants to find some that like acid soil, neutral soil and alkaline soil.

Visit a nearby garden. Back at school, design the kind of garden you would like to have.

Draw a plan of a circular pot and decide how to plant four hyacinth bulbs in it. How far apart are they?

Plant a hyacinth bulb. Measure its growth.

Visit a nearby garden of particular interest or beauty. Draw a map, identifying its key features.

Measure different plants. Measure daily the growth of fast-growing plants, such as runner beans and sunflowers. Keep a chart of their growth.

Investigate the differences between a garden in Cornwall and one in the Highlands of Scotland. Or one in a big city and one in a village.

Vote on what flowers to plant in the school garden.

Design a garden for partially sighted people.

Design a garden for five-year-old children to enjoy.

Design and make a plant book. Include identification keys. Use pressed, dried plants to classify the plants.

Investigate what difference the direction your garden faces makes to decisions on planting. Which bits of the school garden are sunny? Are there bits that never get the sun?

Design a poster describing wildflowers. Include weeds you find around the school. Find out the name of the weeds. Do a survey of weeds around the school.

Survey parents, teachers or other children to find out which is their favourite flower. And least favourite. Put the results in order. Hold a vote to adopt a school flower or plant.

Compare the cost of buying seed, seedlings and fully grown plants. Discuss the pros and cons.

Create a timeline that records key stages in the life of the garden.

Geoboards

Tackle some geoboard challenges. Set out geoboards and rubber bands, with photocopies of an array of pins for children to record their work, and a postbox for answers. Challenges could include: 'Make shapes that touch but don't cross' and 'How many different-sized angles can you make by joining three pins?' Open the box on Friday and give the first correct answer a prize.

g g

Play 'Human geoboards'. Do a geoboard activity on 3 × 3 pinboards. Repeat this on a human board made from nine children standing in rows – use rope instead of rubber bands.

Geography

see also: Calendar, Environment, Food, Gardening, Maps, Money, Trails, Transport, Weather

Geography provides an opportunity to use and draw maps, to explore position and direction, and to handle data. The Maths Week allows children to engage in extended explorations of local geography.

Explore different styles of housing in different countries. Make a presentation using scale drawings and charts.

Investigate how we use water in the school and the home. How can we save it?

Compare populations in different capital cities across Europe.

Research the type of food we eat and where it comes

from. Make a chart of your findings.

Find out where the largest desert in the world is. Which countries contain part of it? How large is it? What lives there? How is life sustained in the desert?

Go for a class walk. Draw a map of where you went and what you saw.

Identify your local shops and produce a chart showing the different types.

Make a large plaque in the playground showing the eight compass directions. Hide some treasure. Mark a starting point, and use compass directions and units of distance to give directions to the treasure.

Make a fingerpost to stand in the playground. Let it point the way to local places of interest: the bank, the hospital, the shopping centre. Or make one to show the direction and distance to Delhi, New York, Paris.

Giant grids

see also: Number lines and tracks

Make giant grids from sheets of A4 card – or carpet tiles – numbered 1 to 100 and lay them out in the form of a 100-grid.

Everyone stands on an even number. What columns are empty of people, and why? What even numbers could you get to by moving one square? Two squares? What addition or subtraction operations would those moves represent?

Everyone chooses a number to stand on, then moves to the number that is 2 more than their original number. Discuss the different movements (some children will go down and left but most will simply move two to the right). Try adding and subtracting different numbers (9, 10 and 11 are interesting). Agree what to do if you go off the grid.

Pairs of children stand on adjacent numbers and find their totals. What happens?

('Sideways' pairs add up to odd numbers and 'downwards' pairs total even numbers.) Why is this?

Pairs of children stand on numbers so that their total is a multiple of 10. What happens? What patterns do you notice?

Everyone chooses a number less than 51 to stand on, then moves to the number that is worth double. How can you get back to where you started?

In groups of four, stand on a 2 × 2 square anywhere on the grid. What is the relationship between your numbers? Is the same relationship true for all the groups? What happens when pairs on the opposite corners add their numbers together? Does the same thing happen for all the groups?

Divide into groups of four (two pairs). Two players stand on 1 and 100.Your partners take turns to roll a dice (marked 1, 2, 3, 9, 10, 11) and tell you how many steps to move – the player on 1 moves towards 100 and the other player moves back towards 1 (so one adds and the other subtracts). The first team to reach the top/bottom row of numbers wins. (Encourage children to take

the 'short cut' for 10 by stepping straight up or down to the next row rather than taking ten steps.)

Two players stand on 1 and 2. Your partners take turns to roll a dice and tell you how many steps to move. If you land on a square number, you move to the next square number; if you land on a prime number, you move back to the previous prime number. At the end, you wait until they roll the right number to reach 100.

Pairs take turns to roll two 0–9 dice and agree whether to add, subtract or multiply the two numbers (or divide, so long as the answer is a whole number). Put bean bags of your team's colour on the answer. The first team to get three in a line wins the game. (Try with three 1–6 dice, whose numbers can be used as single digits or can be combined to make two-digit numbers.)

Greek mathematics

see also: Chinese mathematics, Counting systems, Egyptian mathematics, Vedic mathematics, Zeno's paradox

The Greeks contributed particularly to the

development of geometry in mathematics. Some ideas will be accessible to children. Mathematicians of note include Archimedes, Eratosthenes, Euclid, Hypatia, Pythagoras and Thales.

Research a Greek mathematician in books and on the Internet. Make a presentation about them.

Investigate triangular and square numbers. Use counters to make the first ten triangular numbers and the first ten square numbers. Find out whether it is true that every square number is made up of two triangular numbers.

Use the Sieve of Eratosthenes to find prime numbers to 100. Write up your method.

Halves

see also: Fractions, Mirrors, Number lines and tracks

Finding halves in a range of contexts gives younger children a basis for understanding more complex fractions. In the Maths Week you can make a large display of halves.

Set up a halves table, with objects that one group of children have halved (an orange, a sheet of paper, a bar of chocolate, a square, a stick of cubes). Invite another group to match up the halves to make a whole.

Attempt a domino challenge: using a set of double twelve dominoes, make a loop where the end of every domino matches with one half its value. See how long you can make the loop.

Cut paper shapes in half in different ways. Use them to make a pattern or picture.

Find as many ways as possible of drawing lines to divide a 4 × 4 square grid in half.

Find as many ways as possible of dividing a 3 × 3 geoboard in half with a rubber band.

Find which number under 100 can be halved most often and still give a whole number answer. (The answer is 64; the sequence is 32, 16, 8, 4, 2, 1.)

Hats

see also: Competitions, Festivals, Number lines and tracks

Hats are a useful prop for a range of number games, and a chance for children to be original and creative about mathematical ideas.

Hold a pattern party or assembly: invite all participants to design a patterned hat. Give a prize for each hat. (Invite parents or teachers and support staff and split the prizes into different categories: the tallest hat, the widest, the hat with the most numbers on, the softest… .)

Use hats as props for number songs and rhymes, such as 'Five little speckled frogs' (with frog hats).

Use hats with numbers on, and children have to arrange themselves in number order.

Hold a 'Sorting Hat' competition. Pluck mathematical problems or incomplete calculations out of an impressive hat and sort the players into teams.

Design and parade (or exhibit) a sequence of mathematical hats.

Design and make a maths hat showing a multiplication table.

Design and make a hat based on 3D shapes such as cubes, cylinders, pyramids and cones.

History

see also: Architecture, Calendar, Counting systems, Festivals, Home, Trails, Transport, Vegetables, Victorians, Vikings, Zero

History provides a context for looking at time over a long period, and for data handling. It also offers a way of comparing then and now: costs and money, measures, life style, travel… The Maths Week offers time to run an extended history project.

Make a timeline round the hall showing the different periods of history the school has studied. Bring it up to the present. Add to it significant events from the history of the school.

Hold a poll to find the school's favourite character in history. (Choose your criteria carefully.) Invite Year 6 children to plan the voting system, carry it out and then display the results in tables or charts. Children can present their case to canvass votes.

Work out when the two World Wars started and finished, how long each war lasted, and how long ago that was. How many soldiers died in these wars? And how many civilians?

Research the Leonardo da Vinci designs for early prototypes of helicopters and aircraft.

Research and deliver a presentation on the history of mathematics.

Use the local censuses to find out information about who lived in or near the school, what they did, how long they lived, how large their families were, and so on. Write a report on your conclusions.

Home

see also: Architecture, Design and technology, Geography, Pets, Toys

The mathematics of homes includes measuring, scale drawing, plans and elevations, general problem solving, and data handling. Treat the subject sensitively – children live in very varying circumstances.

Make a plan of your bedroom. Include measurements. Design a new bedroom. Devise a list of items that can be bought, for a budget of £300. Draw the layout of the furniture in your new room.

Design your ideal home. Describe what it would be like to live there.

Use old packaging from white goods to make a home you can fit in.

Plan and then visit the home of a famous historical figure. The planning will include agreeing a timetable for the

day, researching bus routes and working out the cost per person.

Search in the playground for signs of animal homes (a caterpillar on a leaf, a mouse hole, the remains of a bird's nest, ants under a stone). Sketch a plan of the playground, and mark in these homes.

ICT

see also: Languages, Magazine, Money, Music, Needlework, Weather

Many children love hands-on computer work. Plan for them to spend part of their Maths Week playing games, carrying out investigations, adding up, creating databases, painting shapes and patterns — all using computers and other ICT tools. The Internet can be

an important tool, whether for playing games and solving problems or carrying out investigations and mining for data. You could consider an Internet or communications-related theme for the Week.

Set up adventure workshops. Use programs (such as the Zoombinis' *Maths Journey*) that contain mathematical elements.

Use a creative arts package to design a birthday card, a clock face or a class poster. Use a tiling programme to make a repeating pattern for wrapping paper.

Use a spreadsheet to make number patterns or create multiplication tables.

Try out mathematical games and puzzles from websites such as Nrich.

Use SMILE maths games on CD Roms.

Tackle a class maths quiz (prepared on the computer). Take a copy home and do it with your family.

Devise a maths quiz on the computer for your own Year groups or for younger classes.

Play 'Hide and seek' with the floor turtle. Hide an object in the hall or classroom. Take turns to instruct the turtle to make a move; you can tell them whether the turtle is 'warm', 'cold' or 'freezing'.

Teach the floor turtle a simple dance.

Create wrapping paper using ready-made stamps in a graphics package.

Post a maths problem on the school website and invite responses by email.

Design wallpaper, brickwork, and roof tile paper to redecorate the outside of the dolls' house;

work out how many sheets to print out.

Infinity

see also: Zeno's paradox, Zero

Maths Week is an opportunity to explore any aspect of mathematics that you enjoy but that does not quite fit in the normal timetable – such as infinity.

Use a calculator. Start with 1 and keep halving. The calculator will soon give up; suppose you had a magic calculator that didn't. Would you ever stop?

Experiment with infinity. Using a sharp pencil and a ruler, draw a square, mark the midpoints of the sides, and join them up. Mark the midpoints of the new square and repeat. Do this for as long as you can. If you had a really sharp pencil, could you go on for ever?

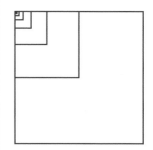

Imagine you are a beetle on a blown-up balloon. What does the balloon look like to you? The balloon gets larger and larger and larger, for ever. What does the balloon look like to you now?

Invent some subtraction problems where the answer is 10. How many are there? Could there be just one more?

What is the highest number? And if you add 1?

Find out how big a googol is (10^{100}). Then add 1.

Investigations

see also: Logic, Magic squares, Zeno's paradox

A Maths Week is an excellent time to carry out investigations, as the open-ended nature of the work, and any uncertainty as to timing, can be accommodated more easily than during a normal week.

Encourage children to extend their investigations, and use this as a chance for children to invent their own problems. Use the technique of 'What if not?' – that is, changing just one aspect of the problem and exploring that. 'You tried it with four cubes: what happens with five?' 'This is how it works with a square: what about a triangle?'

Carry out an investigation, using the Internet as a research tool.

Take a handful of cubes and make them into two sticks (or three towers). Which numbers give you sticks (or towers) of the same length (or height)? Which don't?

Provide interlocking cubes clicked together into sticks. If you had as many 3-sticks and 5-sticks as you liked, what numbers (or lengths) could you make? (Help children formulate their own questions.)

Choose any two odd numbers and add them. Keep doing this. What do you notice about the answers? Why might this be? What happens if you multiply two odd numbers?

Multiply 999 by 1, 2, 3 and so on. What are the patterns that result? Try to find some other number patterns that can be made by multiplying or adding with 9s.

Investigate number palindromes: numbers that are the same backwards (such as 99, 8008, 151). You can form palindromes by reversing the digits of a number and adding the number to its reversal.

$$124 + 421 = 545$$

If this single step doesn't make a palindrome, continue the process until it does.

$$653 + 356 = 1009$$

$$1009 + 9001 = 10010$$

$$10010 + 01001 = 11011$$

Ask younger children to produce some two-digit numbers (or larger) and turn them into palindromes. Invite older children to predict when a number will take more than one step to produce a palindrome – and develop a hypothesis to test.

Jokes

Run a competition and give prizes to the best joke with mathematical content. ('Don't go near seven: seven ate nine'; 'what's 1 and 1? 2 – or is it 11?')

Include a jokes column in the maths magazine.

Journeys

see also: Maps, Outings, Trails, Transport, Walks

A journey can be short or long, literal or virtual.

Program the turtle to go to the secretary's office, so it can take messages for the teacher.

Play, or invent, a board game involving journeys.

Work out how far you walk or run in school during the day. How much of your daily exercise needs does

that fulfil? How far would you walk in a school year?

Plan a journey round the hall that uses some of the PE equipment. Find a way to record this plan using symbols. Try it out during the next PE lesson.

Use a map to find the best route for the outing you have planned for later in the Week.

Juggling

see also: Games, Music

Juggling involves the idea of repeated patterns, a forerunner to algebra.

Invite a circus skills group to hold a juggling workshop.

Write calculations on a large ball. Children stand in a circle and throw the ball from one to another, to music. When the music stops, whoever is holding the ball has to choose a calculation and complete it. (Once done, that calculation cannot be chosen again.)

Learn to play two balls, up in the air and against the wall. Learn some rhymes and sequences for two-ball games:

Oliver, Oliver, Oliver Twist,

Bet you a penny you can't do this.

Bend your knees, stand at ease,

Quick march, over the arch,

Oliver, Oliver, Oliver Twist!

K L Jumping

see also: Physical maths, Sport

Jumping is perfect for time and measure experiments.

Record how many jumps you can do in a minute. Do you make as many in the second minute?

Make jumps of 2 on a giant (or floor) number line. What numbers do you land on if you start at zero? And if you start at 1?

Invent a game to play on a 100-grid or number line that involves making equal jumps.

Investigate whether people with long legs are

better at long jump than people with shorter legs.

K

Kaleidoscope

see also: Mirrors, Reflection, Toys

This classic toy yields itself to exploration of symmetry, pattern and work with mirrors.

Make your own kaleidoscope with mirrors and jewels. Can you make six images? Five? Twelve?

Kites

see also: Construction, Origami

Kites need careful construction if they are to fly and to stay in one piece. Children need help in

experimenting and thinking about how best to design them to become airborne, and what craft techniques to use. Give them free reign in decorating them.

Write a poem with the shape of a kite.

Make kites from cheap or free materials such as garden stakes and newspaper. Or even, for younger children, a piece of paper on a string.

Design a really small kite that can still fly.

Measure the angle your kite is flying at. Use a protractor to the angle of the kite line at the flier's hand, or look along the protractor toward the kite. Which kite flies at the highest angle?

Use a spring gauge to measure the pull of your kite.

Make a 3D kite.

Create a display that shows the designs of the kites you have made.

Hold a working display of kites in the playground

or park or on the field. Hold a Kite Parade to show off your creations. Line everyone up carrying their kites (not flying them), play some music, and march around the room.

L

Languages

see also: Counting systems, Family, Zero

Learn how to count to 10 in ten languages.

Investigate mathematical language. Collect words that have an everyday meaning and a specifically mathematical meaning, such as 'difference', 'full', 'half', 'more' and so on.

Investigate binary language and its connection with computers. How can all numbers be represented by 0 and 1?

Library

see also: Books, History, Trails, Visitors

Let the children's librarian know about the Maths

Week and see whether they have more ideas for library-based activities.

Investigate a topic using the books and materials available in the library.

Ask the librarian in advance of a scheduled visit to look out books with a mathematical theme.

Make your own class library, using homemade books or books brought in from home. Take it in turns to be the librarian. Think about classifications, and the sizes of books and of shelves. If this is a lending library, devise a system for managing this.

Logic

see also: Investigations, Problems and puzzles, Unknown

Logic problems involve unravelling a collection of related statements and working out what conclusions you can draw from these statements. Problems that involve straight reasoning can also be presented as stories. Aristotle devised some in 350 BCE.

Look at the difference between universal statements (no pigs can fly) and existential quantifiers (some cats have tails).

Consider the intriguing problems invented by Lewis Carroll. One of these is: 'deduce the deepest possible conclusion from these three statements:

A. babies are illogical.

B. nobody is despised who can manage a crocodile.

C. illogical persons are despised.'

Introduce children to the writings of Martin Gardner, an American mathematician who writes puzzles, tantalisers and problems (including logic problems) that intrigue some children.

Encourage children to invent their own logic problems.

Magazine

see also: Art and design, English, Jokes, Poems

Devising a maths magazine as an outcome from the Week helps reinforce the link with parents and gives children a tangible product they can take pride in.

This can also be a useful fundraising tool.

Hold a Circa workshop. (Circa is a maths magazine with plenty to interest older primary children.)

Invite each class to contribute a spread to a maths magazine, describing an outcome of their week's activities. Make this an ICT project. Hold a competition to design the front cover. Print a copy of the magazine for each class (or individual child).

Magic

see also: Mazes, Problems and puzzles

There's magic in mathematics.

Make Mobius strips. Use a thick strip of paper and some paper glue. Twist the strip of paper and join the ends in a loop. You will find the loop has only one side and only one edge. Trace round the loop with your finger. Which is the inside and which the outside? Try cutting the strip along its middle. What happens?

Make a Mobius band with two twists. How is it the same, and how does it differ from your original? And with three twists?

Make another band like the first one, and start cutting a third of the way between one edge and the other. Go on until you get back to where you started. What happens? Why?

Tackle some almost impossible challenges. Challenge one: cut a strip of paper more than a metre long from an A4 sheet. (Cut it in a spiral, as though peeling an apple.)

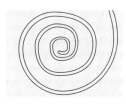

Challenge two: write the number 100 using just four digits, each of which is 9. [$99 + \frac{9}{9} = 100$]

Challenge three: using just three digits, write out a simple addition that totals 24. The digits must all be the same, and can't be 8. [$22 + 2 = 24$]

Perform mathematical magic (in a magician's hat). Ask children if they can work out how and why these pieces of magic work.

Magic trick one: ask the children to choose a 5 × 5 square anywhere within a 100-grid, and draw around it. They briefly show it to you, and you can quickly give them the total of all the numbers in that 5 × 5 square. (You do that by looking for the middle number in the square, and multiplying it by 25 [or multiplying by 100 and halving and halving, if that is easier]).

Magic trick two: invite someone to choose a domino in secret. Then ask them to
• multiply one of the numbers by 2
• add 5 to the answer
• multiply the answer by 5
• add the second number
• subtract 4
Ask them what the final number is. If you silently subtract 21, you will be able to tell them the number of spots on each side of the domino. The numbers are the same as the two digits in that number. (So, if they said '44' and you subtract 21 you are left with 23; the two numbers are 2 and 3.)

Magic squares

see also: **Investigations, Problems and puzzles**

Mark cushions or beanbags or plastic plates with the numbers 1 to 9 and make a grid on the floor with masking tape. Invite children to arrange the numbers in the grid so that every row, every column, and the two diagonals all add to 15.

Use the even numbers (2, 4, 6… 18) and make lines that total 30. (To support younger children, provide crib sheets, where two or three of the numbers are shown in position.)

Make a 4 × 4 magic square. Write the numbers 1 to 16 in order in the squares.

1	2	3	4
5	6	7	8
9	10	11	12
13	14	15	16

Swap the numbers in opposite corners.

16	2	3	13
5	6	7	8
9	10	11	12
4	14	15	1

Swap the numbers in the middle four cells.

16	2	3	13
5	11	10	8
9	7	6	12
4	14	15	1

The rows, columns and diagonals all have the same total now. How else could you arrange the numbers in this magic square, and keep the totals the same?

Mancala

see also: Games

The game of Mancala has been played throughout Africa for thousands of years. Many historians believe it to be the oldest game in the world. As with all ancient games, there are different rules depending on where your family first learned to play. Some people play by scooping out holes in the sand on the beach and using shells; others use beautiful ivory and gold boards.

Organise a Mancala tournament.

Play a game of Mancala using a twelve-hole egg box and 48 cubes.

Maps

see also: Environment, Festivals, Gardening, Geography, Home, Journeys, Outings, Position, School, x-axis

Maps require an understanding of shape, position, angle and movement. Map work can spark off a lifelong love of maps and a desire to discover the world. Use a Peters projection, not the usual Mercator, as the latter distorts the areas taken up by different countries.

Draw a map of different parts of the school: classrooms, the hall, the playground. Display these without labels and challenge someone to identify the various places.

Go on a treasure hunt, with a new clue at each point along the way. Use positional and directional clues ('in the cupboard to

the right of the clock in the hall'). Or use a map, with places marked where there are hidden objects, or special words. Find, and list, all the hidden items.

Display a map of the world. Write your name on a label, stick it at the edge, then join your name to your favourite country (or the one you most want to see), using a drawing pin and thread.

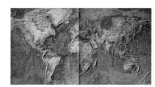

Set up a toy shop or house or farm or garage. Draw a plan of it. Display one or more of the plans, change the scene, and challenge someone to use the plans to spot what has changed.

Mazes

see also: Problems and puzzles, Trails

More ideas for mathematics and mazes are given in *How Amazing* (Charles Snape and Heather Scott). There are also quite a few

websites with information on mazes. Try www.mazes. co.uk, www.longleat.co.uk and www.hrp.org.uk.

Make a maze in the hall, using benches and posts. Children take turns to pretend they are a floor turtle, and follow instructions given orally to negotiate the maze.

Visit a maze. Puzzle your way through a hedge maze, such as Hampton Court or Hatfield House. Test out the rule for getting through mazes: put your right hand against one side of the hedge and follow that edge round until you get to the middle (or the exit). Try this on a paper maze and see if it works.

Design a maze. Make a grid of concentric rectangles, then carefully rub out connections, and draw in blocking walls. Make sure there is a way through, and that there are false paths.

Draw the maze that you have designed on the

playground in chalk for everyone to try.

Invent an adventure game, as a story maze-book of 16 pages. On each page, give a choice about which page to go on to. Before you start, draw a network map of all the connections between the pages, including all the false routes you will set.

Mirrors

see also: Kaleidoscope, Reflection, Symmetry

You can get mirrors made of card covered in a reflective foil. These are perfectly safe, and cheap. Mirror activities could provide part of a workshop on practical maths, or make an interactive display for passers-by to engage with.

Do some mirror writing, then check with a mirror.

Experiment with a pair of mirrors. Put a rubber (or cube or pencil) on the table and use the mirrors to make two, three, four of them. How many can you make? What happens if you use three mirrors?

Draw half a face; make it into a whole face with a mirror.

Take a photograph of your face. Put a mirror down the middle of the photo to turn half your face into a whole face. Does it look like you? Now try with the other half of your face.

Take photographs of objects and their reflections – in rivers, ponds, mirrors, puddles.

Use a mirror and some pictures of people or animals to make strange beasts – or to make them do strange things.

Join three mirrors together, each facing the inside. Use them as a kaleidoscope, moving them over objects, pictures and patterns.

Money

see also: **Citizenship, Drama, Gardening, Outings, Shop**

These activities reinforce children's grasp of financial understanding, financial competence and financial responsibility. Any – or all – of these areas would make a solid theme for the Week.

Change a 0–30 number line into a money line. Stick the coins (1p, 2p, 5p, 10p and so on) under the right numbers. Use the money line to count in 2s: two pence, four pence, six pence…

Collect coins from different countries. What numbers can you find on the coins? Sort the coins by country or value or size, or according to the numbers they show.

Discuss why there is no 3p or 9p coin.

Find out how much different coins weigh.

Make rubbings of coins. Under each rubbing write what the coin is and how much it is worth.

Plan, cost and carry out a class outing. Set a budget. Evaluate whether it was sufficient at the end.

Decide on something worth saving for (for the classroom or for the school as a whole or for a charity). Discuss a means of raising money. Establish a target sheet. Select someone to count and check the money. Monitor progress and announce the results in an assembly.

Compare the cost of something on the Internet.

Invent a board game where you collect money; count up your total at the end.

Find out where money comes from.

Investigate different jobs and salaries. Choose a job. Find out what skills you need for that job. Tell your group about the job and ask someone to interview you to see if you can get it.

Find out how people spend money. Do a survey of the teachers. What conclusions can you reach?

Decide what you would do with £50 (£100, £500). Why?

Play 'Make £1' in groups of two to five players (from Years 2 to 4). Take turns to roll the money dice (marked 1p, 2p, 2p, 5p, 5p, 10p). Take from the money bag whichever coin the dice tells you to. When everybody has reached a total of £1 or more the game is over.

Play 'Aim for 100' in groups of two to four players (from Years 2 to 4). You need a 100-grid, a counter each, and a bag of coins. Take turns to pick a coin from the bag and say its value. Move your counter that number of spaces along the 100-grid. (For example, if you get 5p you move five squares.) Whoever reaches 100p (£1) first, is the winner.

Play 'Make the Most' in groups of two to five players (from Years 2 to 4). You need two sets of money cards, one set showing multiples of 10p (10p, 20p, 30p… 90p) and one showing multiples of 1p (1p, 2p, 3p… 9p). Shuffle the two sets of cards and put each one face down. Each player takes a card from each set and finds the total. Whoever has the highest total is the winner.

Play 'Spending money' in groups of two to four players (from Years 2 to 4). This game is like 'Aim for 100' but it's about spending money. One player is the banker, so can use a calculator to check calculations with; nobody else can. Take a £1 coin each and place your counters on 100. In turn, roll a dice to tell you how much money to spend, and how many spaces to move towards the beginning. Decide what you are spending it on, and say what it is. Then tell the banker how much change you need; the banker must give you the right change, even if you told them the wrong amount. Whoever spends all their money last is the winner.

Play 'Aim for £2' in groups of two to three players (from Years 2 to 4). You need plenty of 10p, 5p and 1p coins. Take turns to roll a 1–6 dice and take that many coins; they must all be the same denomination (all 10p or 5p or 1p coins). Keep track of your score. You can drop out of the game whenever you choose. When you have all finished, whoever is closest to £2 wins.

Investigate the difference between cash and 'plastic' forms of money. Define the difference between credit and debit. Design a poster describing your findings.

Music

see also: Drama, Festivals, Patterns, Up

Music and mathematics are natural partners, giving rise to some delightful activities.

Follow symbols in a music session to indicate which instrument(s) should be played. How is this similar to (and different from) the way we read symbols in mathematics? Choose a conductor to point to the symbols in sequence. (The players have to produce sound until the next symbol is indicated.) Create your own sequence of sounds and then write it down, using the symbols, so that you can play each other's music at a later date.

Talk about the mathematics of square dancing: opposite partners across the diagonal of a square of four dancers; going clockwise and anti-clockwise round the room and the circle; changing direction with your partner; weaving alternately through the line; remembering a repeated sequence in a particular dance.

Hold a square dancing session. Square dancing music is in eight-bar groups, with a sequence of 32 bars. Invent a square dance with a repeated sequence of eight moves, arriving back at the beginning again. Can you find a way of recording a particular dance sequence on paper? Invent a notation for the patterns of exchanging partners in a reel of four.

Compose a times table rap to help you learn a multiplication table.

Compose and record music on a computer.

Make an octave scale using milk bottles with different levels of water in them. (How are you going to make sure the notes are right?) Plot a graph of the volume of water in the bottle against the note of the bottle when struck.

What can you say about the graph?

Visit a church organ. Find out what the numbers on each stop mean. How does an eight-foot stop sound compared with a four-foot or two-foot stop? What would a 32-foot stop sound like, or a 64-foot stop?

Sing number songs and rhymes.

Listen to music that uses repeated patterns and clap in time.

Investigate whether your heart rate increases when you listen to music with a fast beat.

Needlework

see also: Patterns, Quilts, Shapes

A needlework session gives children the chance to

practise repeating a pattern of movements; using a sense of 3D space; measuring; following complicated symbolic instructions; and imagining how 2D and 3D shapes fit together. Bring in experienced practitioners of knitting, crochet, weaving and embroidery to teach the children. Encourage children to notice the mathematical words they use: 'over', 'under', 'behind', 'count', 'long' and so on.

Design, make and test a set of templates for patchwork. Use Logo to help with the design. Or use different mathematical grid paper or plastic shapes. Start with very simple ideas and shapes!

Make cross stitch patterns. Use graph paper to work out the design of a simple motif. Now use that motif by repeating it, and by making symmetrical patterns. Make a strip pattern with your motif on binca fabric. Make a rectangular pattern with a border and a symmetrical motif in the centre.

Negative numbers

see also: Infinity, Number lines and tracks, Zero

Play 'Either side of zero'. Twenty children form pairs; each pair has a number from 1 to 10. Both partners write this on a sheet of A4 paper or card, then one makes it positive and one negative (by adding a + or − at the front). Put a large zero on a chair and arrange yourselves in order on either side of it. The children who are there as observers answer questions about the number line, then swap places with one of the children in the line.

Invent a game using a negative/positive number track (for example, from −15 to +15). Base it around a real-life scenario that models the positive/negative aspect, such as diving, rock-climbing, pot-holing, or temperature. Present the games at an open event.

Nets

see also: Shapes, Squares

Look at a display of some nets on squared paper – some will fold up to make cubes and some won't. Which ones will work?

Make nets of other solids using isometric (triangular) or squared paper, and fold them into the solid shape. Don't forget the tabs. Make giant ones to colour and hang from the ceiling.

Number lines and tracks

see also: Cards, Giant grids, Jumping, Money, Negative numbers, Up

Now is your moment to try things on a larger scale, for instance with a large floor number line or track.

Make a floor number line to 10 or 20 using chalk or masking tape straight on the floor. Or make a number line on a roll of transparent plastic carpet protector. Make floor number tracks from numbered carpet tiles.

These games and activities work better with a pair or group than with a whole class.

Number lines commonly start at zero and have space between the numbers for fractional numbers; tracks are more like a row of numbers on a 100-square. If you want to include zero in your activity, use a number line rather than track.

Place the cards zero and 10 (or 20) at opposite ends of an unnumbered line. Figure out where to place the rest of the cards. Discuss which number to place first and why.

Place the half numbers on the line. Practise taking steps along it.

Use a 1–10 number track. One child stands on 'start' and the others sit beside the track. Give someone a number card from 5 to 10: they read out the number and the child on the number track takes that many steps forwards. Guess how many more steps they will need to take to reach 10. The child on the track takes the remaining steps to 10 while everybody counts. Were your guesses correct?

Put groceries at every number on the 0–10 track. Two children, each with a basket, stand at 'start'. Their partners take turns to roll a 1–3 dice, and instruct them to take that number of steps. Wherever they stop, they take the grocery item to put in their basket. They continue moving up and down the line until there are no goods left.

Put hats at several numbers on the 1–20 track. Two children, wearing hats, stand at 'start'. Their partners take turns to roll a 1–3 dice, and instruct them to take that number of steps towards 10 (or 20). If they stop on a hat, they swap their hat for that one.

Origami

see also: Art and design, Nets, Shapes

Origami is the Japanese art of paper-folding, following a sequence of diagrams. There are conventions about showing how and which way to fold, which side of the paper is which, and what the three-dimensional shape looks like. Reading these help children with 2D and 3D shape, and with position and direction. They can also invent their own folds and shapes, and represent these in diagrammatic instructions. Origami requires precise folding, in halves, quarters and thirds. You can analyse the creases by undoing an origami shape and imagining what it could fold up into.

Make gift boxes to hold biscuits you have baked.

Make creatures and objects that fit in with other themes of the week: insects, dinosaurs, vehicles, fruit.

Outings

see also: Environment, Gardening, History, Trails, Walks

Any outing needs to be planned well in advance. Decide whether – and how much – to involve children in the planning.

Write a detailed timetable for a day out locally.

Use bus timetables to work out a bus trip – include waiting times at bus stops, and times taken for buses to reach destinations.

Work out how much an outing is likely to cost.

Use the scale on a large-scale Ordnance Survey map and thin string (or thick thread) to measure the distance you are going to travel.

Visit a museum. Divide into teams (of three or four) to complete a worksheet. Back at school, write up your findings for a 'letter home' or class poster.

Visit an art gallery to study shape, space and pattern. Put drawings into a class scrapbook, with captions. Display the scrapbook in the reception area.

Visit another primary school. Conduct a survey of the children's likes and dislikes and produce a report that compares what you find with your school.

Visit a residential home. Investigate its disabled access facilities. Could they be better? Give the residents a performance.

Go to a public building. Identify its main features. Find out how much it costs to run the building.

Visit a secondary school. Investigate how maths is taught in this school.

Visit a café. How do they cost their meals?

Patterns

see also: Art and design, Festivals, ICT, Kaleidoscope, Music, Needlework, Reflection, Shapes, Symmetry, Tessellation, Vikings, Weaving

Algebraic thinking begins when you can express patterns in words, pictures and symbols, and can make generalisations about them. Spotting patterns when you are sorting, recognising visual patterns, enjoying rhythm and movement, and making connections, is the basis for algebra.

Enjoy sequence rhymes, such as 'The old lady that swallowed a fly', 'The house that Jack built', 'Green grow the rushes oh' and 'In my bag I packed'. Now make up your own sequence rhyme.

Use pegboards: make patterns that repeat in one direction or two, symmetrical patterns, patterns using two colours or three, and a pattern of squares that get bigger.

Use different objects to make necklaces showing a repeating pattern or a symmetrical one. Hide part of the necklace. What pieces are hidden?

Make growing or shrinking patterns with counters, or print them with pencil stubs, or colour them in on squared paper. Look at the number pattern that goes with the visual one; talk about what the next numbers would be.

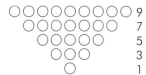

```
○○○○○○○○○  9
 ○○○○○○○    7
  ○○○○○      5
   ○○○        3
    ○          1
```

Make square 'flower beds' of increasing size using square tiles to form the paths round the 'beds'. Look at the number patterns and talk about how they grow.

Explore possibilities. 1, 2, 3, 5, 8, 13, 21... How might this continue?

Display a set of 'Think of a number...' problems. Challenge people to spot the pattern that makes the problem work. For example: Think of a number, double it, add the number you first thought of, double the result, add the number you first thought of. Divide this number by 7, and you end up with the number you first thought of.

Pets

see also: Family, Home, Science

Featuring pets as part of a Maths Week provides lots of opportunity for data collection as well as bringing children's outside lives into school.

Hold a whole school investigation into the pets people have in their families. Collect data on what animals they look after, the sort of food their pets eat and how much it costs to buy.

Hold a pet weigh-in. Find the heaviest cat and the lightest cat, as well how much most cats weigh. Find the tallest and the shortest dog, the hamster with the largest waist measurement and the slimmest hamster. Collect and display all the information that has been submitted, using a range of media including photos of particular pets, such as the smallest mouse and the largest guinea pig. Put together a display of a week's food eaten by a gerbil and compare it with the amount eaten by a fish.

Collect data on the most popular name for a pet and involve the children in the design and organisation of the data. Find out and generalise about 'who walks our dog' and 'where our cat sleeps' as well as 'who cleans out the rabbit hutch'. Discuss the results and your conclusions.

Physical maths

see also: Construction, Geoboards, Giant grids, Juggling, Jumping, Number lines and tracks, Time, Up

During the Week, plan to do maths on a large scale, with children moving around and physically acting out the mathematics.

Build skeletal 3D shapes using metre-long sticks and joiners. Make part of a geodesic dome with triangles, or an octahedral structure, or a tetrahedron.

Draw a circle using string and chalk. Stand on one spot and ask your partner to pull the string straight

and mark out the circle on the ground. Investigate the ratio between the length of string and the circumference of the circle.

Mark out the x and y axes and the coordinates in chalk on the playground. Choose someone to call out coordinates. The others have to work out where to stand on the grid.

Use string to make large polygons in the playground. Three children hold the strings as the corner of a triangle. Four children make a quadrilateral.

Wear number cards (using pins or shoulder straps) and arrange yourselves in order, or as odd and even numbers, or as multiples of 5, or all those more than 2 and less than 8.

Estimate long distances in the playground. Pace them out, then measure them. Try and improve the estimates with practice.

Playground

see also: **Games, Gardening, Home, Physical maths, School, Trees**

Use the Maths Week as an opportunity to reassess the use of the playground.

Do a litter survey of the playground each day.

Decide what to do to solve the litter problem, and put the plan into action.

Create a garden. Set aside a part of the playground for the garden. Plan everything beforehand.

Analyse the use of the playground, and plan to make a better and safer place to play. Plan how to do the surveys, how to present the information, and how to draw conclusions from it.

Poems

see also: **English, Environment, Kites, Magazine**

Listen to and make up number rhymes, such as 'one/fun; two/few; three/sea'. Write a poem using the rhymes.

Write a poem that fits a shape (such as a triangle).

A
boy
swam
silently
along the
flowing river

Write a poem that follows the edges of a shape (such as a spiral or a circle).

one song singing, two birds flying, three children laughing, four cats crawling through the undergrowth towards you

Write a poem where the first line is one word, the second line two words, the third three words and so on, up to the tenth line (ten words).

Choose your favourite poem from a specially selected set (to do with number, shape, measure, weight or time) and read it to the group or the rest of the class.

"I should", says the vampire, and glowers,

"Get a clock showing TWENTY-FOUR hours.

Now I've woken at noon

It's twelve hours too soon –

In the daylight I lose all my powers!"

(a poem by A Stanton as part of Numberland for Maths Year 2000)

Explore Numberland on the 'Count on' website (www.counton.org).

Include a feature on maths poems in the newsletter or the school maths magazine.

Position

See also: **Geoboards, Maps, Origami, Reflection, Trails**

Hide an object in the room, or playground. Describe where it is, while others search for it. Talk about and record the useful words for describing position: 'under', 'near', 'next to'.

Roll a cube onto a large sheet of paper. Describe where it is. Do the same on a large sheet of squared paper. Which task was easier? Why?

Put a single peg in a pegboard and ask children to describe where it is. Put several pegs in, and ask children to choose one and describe its position to you so you can identify it.

Draw treasure maps and decide where to place the buried treasure – don't mark the spot on the map: use coordinates to describe its position instead.

Locate your school or home on a local map or aerial photograph.

Chalk compass directions onto the playground. Choose an object in the playground as a target. Work out how you can get there from the school door using these directions. Swap with a partner, and try to locate and identify their object.

Problems and puzzles

see also: **Chess, Dominoes, Investigations, Mazes, Tangrams, Unknown, Zeno's paradox**

Problem solving is at the core of mathematical activity: it is the context in which children apply their mathematical understanding, knowledge and skills. Often, problem solving is contained within

the mathematics lesson. The Maths Week provides an opportunity for children to do extended problems and investigations, and to invent their own problems.

If the ragdoll has two hats and three tops, none the same, how many different outfits can it wear?

What do you think?
A jeweller says she can balance any lump of gold from 1 gram up to 40 grams with these weights: 1 g, 3 g, 9 g, 27 g. Is she right?

How many complete squares can you draw round a 2 × 2 square grid without lifting your pencil off the paper? You may cross a line you've drawn but not draw along the same line twice. What happens on a 3 × 3 grid? A 4 × 4 grid? Larger grids?

Imagine a language that only had three letters to spell its words. How many different words could it spell? What if it had four or five letters?

Which of the following statements are true or false?
True or false?
44 is a square number

21 is a triangular number

The product of 5 and 3 is 8

The sum of 17 and 18 is 35

23 subtracted from 39 is 26

235 expressed to the nearest 100 is 300

235 expressed to the nearest 10 is 240

The value of the digit 6 in the number 3654 is 600

5 squared is 10

The factors of 24 are 1, 2, 3, 4, 6, 8, 12, 24

441 is an even number

104 is divisible by 4

Invent your own set of 'true or false?' statements.

Your friend has stuck together some wooden cubes to make a larger cube (3 × 3 × 3). How many cuts would you need with a saw to separate all the cubes again?

How many hours have you been alive?

Work out the remainder on division by 5 of each number in the 3 times table. What do you notice

about the remainders? What happens with other tables and divisors?

Can you get 60 as an answer by multiplying only prime numbers together? Try finding numbers that are the products of primes.

Make an open-topped box with the largest possible capacity, using a sheet of A4 paper or card.

Would you rather have your height in a pile of pennies, or your width (fingertip to fingertip) in 20p coins put edge to edge?

Choose a shoe from the box. How big is the person who wears the shoe? Make a life-size model or drawing of them.

Investigate the value of your friends' names, if each letter of the alphabet has a value. A is 1, B is 2, and so on.

Make up your own problems like these.

Quiet time
see also: Books, Investigations

Schedule in quiet time for extending problems and investigations, for reading and reflecting.

Quilts
see also: Needlework, Shapes

Quilts invite children to visualise shapes, analyse the characteristics of shapes, and work out how to dissect and reassemble them. You can design quilts and recreate them with coloured paper or sticking fabric, rather than sewing.

Design tiling quilts tessellating one shape, or using two or more different polygons to cover the surface without overlapping. Use geometric mosaic floor patterns as inspiration (or contemporary architecture and design).

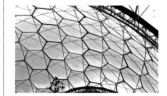

Make an exhibition of quilt patterns from around the world.

Use right-angled triangles to design a quilt. Spiral right-angled triangles on their own or with squares.

Make spiral quilts, using features of buildings or natural objects such as shells, horns and sunflowers as inspiration.

Quiz
see also: Calculators, Competitions, ICT, Television

To avoid causing difficulties for individual children, ask them to work in pairs or teams, or set a choice of easy and hard questions.

Set multiple choice questions and run a short, speedy quiz.

Were candle clocks first used 100 years ago, 1000 years ago or 1 million years ago?

The triangular numbers start 1, 3, 6, 10. Is the next one 15, 16 or 20?

p Q

Human beings have chromosomes in their cells. Does every cell have 3, 12 or 46 chromosomes?

Reflection

see also: Kaleidoscope, Mirrors, Pattern, Position, Shapes

Reflection is an aspect of the movement and position element of shape and space. Shapes can be reflected in mirrors or any 'shiny surface' or in virtual mirrors. Shapes reflected in one mirror line produce another shape with mirror or reflective symmetry.

Look through the mirror. Stand facing your friend and pretend there is a mirror between you. Take it in turns to make a shape with your body. Your partner pretends to be your 'mirror image'

Can you do a mirror dance where every move you make is 'reflected ' by your partner?

Read the Mirror books by Marion Walter. Make up your own book like *Make a bigger puddle*.

Make a reflection of a reflection. Use two mirrors hinged together with masking tape. Stand them up on the table and put a 1p coin between them. How much money can you see when you look into the mirrors? What is the most (or least) amount of money you can see by changing the angle of the mirrors?

How does a kaleidoscope work?

Make distorted mirrors. Use reflective surfaces which distort your image when you look into them, such as plastic mirrors that can be bent, spoons, a stainless steel kettle or wing mirrors.

Remainders

see also: Calculators, Fractions

Play the remainders game using number cards. Take turns to pick a card (from 10 to 50) and roll a 1–6 dice; divide the card number by the dice number: the score is the remainder. The first player to score 30 points wins.

Play the remainders game using a 100-grid. Pick any number on the grid, roll a 1–10 dice and divide the first number by the other, scoring the remainder. You can't use that number on the grid again.

Challenge older children to work out how to find the remainder when dividing on a calculator. The first one to come up with the correct procedure explains it to the others and sets some problems as practice.
$9 \div 4 = 2 \cdot 25$.
There are two 4s in 9. To find the remainder, take the decimal part of the number and multiply it by the number after the division sign.
$0 \cdot 25 \times 4 = 1$.

Right angles

see also: Rotation, Shapes

Find twenty different things with right angles somewhere in the school.

Make right angles with your bodies; take turns to draw each other's shape.

Collect objects that can be turned (a jam jar and lid, door handle, clock hands) and practise turning them

through a right angle, less than a right angle, and more than a right angle.

Rotation

see also: Physical maths, Position, Rotational symmetry, Shapes

A 'circular' movement, rotation is movement in a clockwise or anticlockwise direction around a point. It is an aspect of the movement and position element of shape and space, and can be linked to points of the compass.

Turn through the compass. Start by facing any specified direction, such as North. Then turn through quarter, half or full turns. Which way are you facing? What can you see? How far do you have to turn to see the tree at the end of the playground?

Play circle games like "Ring o' Roses", changing direction from clockwise to anti-clockwise.

Make a display of objects that rotate, such as lids on jars, spinning tops, a kitchen whisk, scissors, door handles, and so on.

Play 'Simon says', and include turning to the left, or to the right, or all the way round.

Rotational symmetry

see also: Rotation, Shapes, Symmetry

This is a property of a shape or pattern such that if you turn the shape it will fit into its own outline in different numbers of ways. A square is said to have an order of rotational symmetry of 4 and a circle an order of rotational symmetry of infinity.

Find shapes. Make a display of shapes that have only rotational symmetry. Extend your search to the environment; include things like wheel hubs, recycling signs and road signs.

Make shape patterns. Use some asymmetrical shapes like a scalene triangle to create a pattern that has rotational symmetry.

Use a spirograph to create a rotationally symmetrical pattern.

Rubbish

see also: Environment, Food, Home

Investigating rubbish gives an interesting context for data handling. Re-using rubbish as art materials gives experience of shapes and their relation to each other. Work with parents to find sources of 'rubbish' that you can re-use for art, design and technology, and for general use. Prepare a collection of this material before the Maths Week.

Research how litter is handled in your school. Make a collection of litter in the school playground. Record the kind of litter that is dropped, where it is found, where the bins are located, the time of day (or week) when the bins are emptied and the direction of the prevailing wind. Is there a problem with litter in your school? If you think it's serious, plan a publicity campaign using posters.

Do a survey of the rubbish created by a household in one day. Decide how much of the rubbish is recyclable and how much has to be thrown away permanently. Investigate what happens to rubbish. Find out how recycling works, and about landfills and incineration. What is the rubbish disposal policy of the local council? Can you make recommendations to your school about the effective use of rubbish?

Create an art exhibition of collage and sculpture from found objects. Choose a theme, like parallelograms, or time.

Read *Stig of the Dump* (Clive King). Follow it up with work on 2D and 3D shape, and construction activities. What could you create if you lived in a rubbish dump?

Read *The Borrowers* (Mary Norton). Then watch the film. Draw pictures of the characters and their home (or make a model). Discuss proportion.

School

see also: History, Maps, Outings, Playground

Use your own school as a focus for the Maths Week, and find out unexpected things about it.

Find the school on a map of the area and trace your route home. Compare the map with an aerial photograph.

Make a class book showing all the different shapes of window in the school, and display it outside the classroom.

Prepare a presentation to everyone of amazing facts about the school: how many bricks (roughly) it contains; how old it is in days; how thick the walls are in millimetres; how many litres of water would fit in a classroom (and how many goldfish could live comfortably in there) … .

Organise a treasure hunt around the school for another class. Work out how much to spend on treasure, and how to spend it; how to organise the hunt, and how to make it safe. Check your plan before carrying it out.

Make a model of the school.

Science

see also: Environment, Food, Surveys, Trails, X-rays

Hold a Maths and Science Week and make explicit the maths used in science. Focus on data handling, measurement, distances and changes over time.

Hold a guessing competition about melting ice. Plan where to put ice cubes – on the radiator, an outside windowsill or in a cupboard. Write down predictions about how long each will take to melt. Observers record the time taken for each one, and

whoever's estimates are closest win prizes.

Collect snails. Do all snails have the same markings? Investigate their speeds. Wake a sleepy snail up with a spray of clean water (it will think it is raining and will come out of its shell). Once it is on the move, transfer it to a wet ruler. Note the number where its head end is, and start timing it. Note the number where the snail ends up. Experiment further by using different surfaces.

Sort, classify and arrange collections. Invent classification keys to help identify your collections.

Count the number of bones in the human body. And in a bird.

Pour 50 ml of water onto the same-sized squares of blotting paper, plastic sheeting, writing paper and cardboard. Record what you see, and observe the differences over time.

Discuss what will happen to the water when a litre is poured onto the (dry) playground. Discuss the measuring you can do, and the measuring instruments you will need; then try it.

Invent your own egg race competition for the week.

Investigate the melting point of chocolate; research the maths involved in finding out what it is. Learn to read thermometer scales, then start the experiment…

Shapes

see also: Architecture, Design and technology, Festivals, Geoboards, Hats, Kites, Origami, Physical maths, Quilts, Reflection, Rotational symmetry, Spirals, Squares, Symmetry

Explore patterns and shapes in the local built environment.

Collect food packets and identify their shapes – tin of beans (cylinder), tea packet (cuboid), stock cube box (cube). Make giant replicas – or miniature ones.

Hold a Shape workshop. Set challenges using construction sets such as Polydron. Make 3D shapes with mathematical beer mats. Make skeletal shapes with straws and pipe cleaners. Fold and weave shapes. Play Edward de Bono games, and do 3D jigsaw puzzles. Make models with junk boxes. Print patterns with shape stamps.

Make a cube dice big enough to get inside.

Use garden canes to make a skeleton cube that could fit a million 1 cm cubes. (This would be a metre cube – one with all its edges one metre long.)

Stick string onto card in the shape of a spiral. When it's dry, take rubbings from it.

Put various flat or 3D shapes in a feely bag and

seal the end. Have a competition to identify the shapes. (As a help for younger children provide pictures of the shapes in the bag, plus some extras, and ask them to identify which of the pictures match shapes inside the bag.)

Make your own posting box for a range of shapes. How many shapes can go through the same hole? How many holes do you need to cut out to post a cube? A cylinder?

Hold a Triangle Hunt in the school or along the street. Make paper triangles, and learn to recognise them in all orientations, then go round looking for things that are that shape. Or look for circles or squares.

Shop

see also: Café, Money, Vegetables

As well as all the activities that exist around the theme of shopping, the Maths Week provides a chance to run a shop: this could be a maths shop, a bookshop, an arts and crafts shop, a pet shop or a cake shop.

Set up a maths shop, selling bought-in books of maths puzzles and games. Sell dominoes, calculators, dice, rulers and protractors, and games to go with them.

Grow plants from seedlings (or bring some from home, or visit a garden centre) and sell them after school.

Hold a sale of second-hand or homemade items. Vote for what to spend the proceeds on. Arrange items into boxes or on tables according to price – a 2p table, a 10p table, and so on. Plan a rota for minding the stalls at the sale.

Help restock the play shop in the reception class. Make food items from playdough; fill food packages with paper and

stick on price labels; design new £5 and £10 notes, then photocopy them.

Visit a market. Imagine everybody has £5 to spend on a nutritious meal for two. Plan how to spend it. What stalls are there, and what kinds of stall are missing? Do a survey to find out what new stalls people would like included.

Investigate how much weight a plastic shopping bag can hold without breaking. Test different materials.

Size

see also: Architecture, Body measures, Construction

Make a stick figure (using strips of card) that is a quarter (or half) as tall as you.

Put some 10 cm sticks on the OHP and work out how many times the image of the sticks is enlarged when it appears on the screen. Are 5 cm sticks enlarged the same amount?

Make a cube from some smaller cubes, and hide a special cube with stars on in the middle.

Make a set of nesting boxes.

Make a loop of string 30 cm long. Arrange it on squared paper – what is the largest number of squares it can enclose?

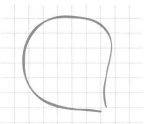

Hold a Size workshop, with an activity on each table. Be the shoemaker (from the folk tale) and make a set of clothes for the elves. Make a model of the table that is one tenth the size. Make a

shape twice the size of this shape, then describe how it is twice the size. Design, cut out and make a pair of trousers that are the right size for you. Use cubes to make a model of a dog twice as big as this one.

Spirals

see also: **Clay, Poems, Shapes**

A spiral is a type of curve. It can be constructed by making a line that moves steadily away from or towards a fixed point. Children meet various types of spiral, some during day-to-day experiences, for example a spider's web, cockle shells and springs.

Construct spirals using different materials. (Establish that within each spiral there is a fixed point from which a curved line or 3D construction moves away with increasing distance.)

Create a spiral using playdough in the form of a long sausage. Leave a gap

between the curves. Drop a marble into the outer edge and watch as it traces a spiral route to the centre.

Construct a 3D spiral (helix) by rolling a sheet of paper about a corner and looking at the pathway the edge of the paper takes. Try rolling a piece of paper at right angles to one edge. Pull the paper out from the centre of the roll to create a 3D spiral.

Collect objects and pictures that depict spirals. Feel, trace and discuss these.

Make square spirals, using Lego on a baseboard or multilink on squared paper.

Construct a spiral on squared paper. Choose a fixed starting point and plot:
right 1
right 2
right 3
right 4
right 5
right 6
right 7
right 8
right 9

Talk about the spiral. What would happen to the spiral if each step was increased by 1? Or if each step was doubled? Or if it was drawn on a triangular grid?

Make a three-step spiral by repeatedly plotting:
right 3
right 4
right 5

Use colour in your spiral to create patterns.

Create spirals from lengths of rope or ribbon arranged on the ground. Invite someone to walk along your spiral.

Sport

see also: **Body measures, Games, Journeys, Playground**

Sport can involve position and movement, time and distance, data handling and problem solving. Involving children in the organisation, and the invention, of sports, means they will need to think about timing, team rotas,

space constraints, ground markings, sequences, and so on. Bear in mind that children often prefer team events to individual competition.

Hold a contest to discover the fastest runner in the class. Or the slowest walker – stick to the rule that contestants must keep moving.

Set up a rota for a keep-going marathon. A group of four or five take turns tossing the ball to each other, but every minute one person drops out and another steps in. How long can the team keep going without dropping the ball?

Organise relay races, a tug of war, or small-scale team games.

Invent a four-a-side team game, using some small apparatus (such as bats, balls, beanbags or skittles). Write down the rules for others to play. What could improve the game?

Do the same loop card round every day, timing it exactly. How much quicker do you all get over the week? Compete with other classes, not to beat their quickest time, but to reduce your own time by the greatest amount.

Squares

see also: **Music, Nets, Rotational symmetry, Shapes**

Make lots of different square picture frames with linking cubes; investigate how the number of cubes increases with the size of the frame.

Find out how many 1 cm squares there are in a one-metre square.

Do some activities with squared paper. Cut out a square (say 8 × 8 or 13 × 13), tear off its corner and ask a partner to work out how many squares there were in the original. Or make a pattern by colouring the squares, then ask a friend to

continue it. Or cut out as many different-sized squares as you can, then put them in order of size.

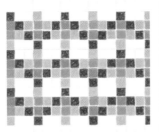

Make different-sized cubes and cuboids.

Make the net of a cube from squared paper. How many different nets can you make that work?

Hold a Square Day. Wear something with a square on it; write on square (or squared) paper; make square shapes with a partner in PE; bake square cakes or flans; explore what shapes you can make with square Clixi pieces…

Make a 100-grid – but choose a rectangle not a

10 × 10 square to make it on. What number patterns can you find in it?

Learn some square dancing; draw the path you move through in the dance.

Surveys

see also: **Architecture, Citizenship, Environment, Food, Gardening, Geography, Money, Pets, Playground, Rubbish, Shop, Television, Vegetables, Victorians, Weather, You**

Surveys work best when their purpose is clear and interesting to children. You may already have a reason for a survey; if not, be alert for news of any interesting nationwide surveys taking place during the Week.

Survey the volume of traffic outside the school. To back up your request to the council for traffic calming in your street, survey the traffic's speed.

Do a rain survey for the Week. Put a measuring cylinder outside, where it won't get blown over, and away from places where trees or buildings keep the rain off. Check its contents at the same time every day; record results on a graph. Do another survey at another time of year, or at the same time next year, to give a point of comparison.

Symmetry

see also: **Art and design, Festivals, Kaleidoscope, Mirrors, Patterns, Rotational symmetry, Transport, Vegetables, Weaving**

Fold sticky paper squares in half and cut out a pattern, then unfold them. Combine all the squares to make a patchwork quilt and display it in the hall.

Make symmetrical faces by folding A4 paper in half and cutting out half a face, then unfolding. Make a display. Make another display of faces where each has been cut along its line of symmetry and joined to a non-matching half. Which half belongs where?

Find examples of symmetry around your school.

Perform a mirror routine, working in pairs. (Rehearse first.) Agree where the large imaginary mirror is, then position yourself in front of it and do some movements. Your partner mimics these movements as if they were your reflection.

Look at symmetry in art.

Work out how many lines of symmetry are needed to form a Rangoli pattern. Invent your own.

Tangrams

see also: **Problems and puzzles, Shapes**

Use the pieces of a tangram to create a picture (a 'house', a 'car' or a 'giraffe'). Trace over the picture and cut out the outline. Display each outline mounted on black paper. Invite other children to work out how the tangram was created from the pieces. (Provide tangram pieces in card for children to use when trying to recreate these pictures.)

Look at photocopies of a tangram. Explore what fraction of the whole each piece is. Cut up the tangram and compare actual pieces.

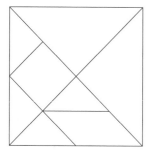

Television

see also: **Home, You**

Investigating TV-watching gives scope for timetables and data handling.

Do a survey of how many hours a week people watch television. Compare this with how much time they spend asleep or at school.

Plan ahead. Next week you can only watch ten hours of television. Look at the listings and then decide your week's viewing. Display your results as a timetable, showing the start and finish times of the programmes.

Time the advertising slots. What proportion of the viewing time do they take up in one hour? List ten adverts broadcast between 6 pm and 7 pm and classify them according to product: cars, sweets, shampoo… . Compare this with adverts broadcast at other times of day.

Find out the top six favourite television programmes in the school.

Write and perform a TV advert that will take exactly one minute to show.

Invent a mathematical television quiz or game show, and try it out with the class. Ask for feedback; keep trying to improve it.

Tessellation

see also: **Architecture, Patterns, Quilts, Shapes**

Use Logo to investigate whether all triangles or quadrilaterals tessellate.

Draw round a square or triangle template; design a tiling pattern that covers a sheet of paper. Try to make a different pattern to others using the same shape.

Look around the school for examples of tessellation and record them. Make a display, and challenge children to identify where in the school these patterns are from.

Explore the reason why all quadrilaterals tessellate. Use the Escher rule of changing one side of a quadrilateral and sliding that change to the opposite side, and fixing it there. Can you make this work with triangles?

Time

see also: **Calendar, Gardening, Jumping, Physical maths, Trees, Up, Visitors, You**

There are two distinct aspects to time. One is a point in time: What time is it? What day or year is it? The other is duration of time: How long will it take? How many days or years was it? Involve children in both of these during the Week. Events will need to be timetabled at specific times and days, and they will also need to last a particular length of time.

Teach your partner (one of the younger children) how to tell the time – or at least how to tell the hours and half hours.

Make a simple sundial. On a bright day stand in the same place in the playground every hour. Ask someone to draw round your shadow with chalk each time. Mark the hour on the head of your shadow. Use this sundial to tell the time on subsequent days. Or make a sundial by sticking a pencil into plasticine and mounting that on a square of wood. Mark the shadows throughout the day.

Invent a water alarm clock with a bell and a battery. The water drips into the container. When the level reaches the disconnected wires the bell rings.

Construct a Chinese water clock, with leaking yoghurt pots one above the other on a stand. Adjust the holes in the pots and the number of pots to make the clock run faster or slower.

Make a collection of home egg-timers. Do all the egg-timers take the same time to empty? Which is the fastest and which is the slowest?

Use a five-minute sand-timer to measure how long playtime is.

Collect a variety of candles. Use these to make a range of candle clocks. How long does the birthday candle take to burn? Use identical candles and find out how to calibrate them. Stick pins in a candle at equal intervals, light the candle, and listen for when they drop down on to a tin lid. Can you calibrate another candle for each quarter or half an hour?

Design a clock face with the hours marked in Roman numerals.

Make a pendulum clock. Try changing the length. Now try changing the weight. Do these affect the timing? Make a salt pendulum by suspending a squeezy bottle filled with salt upside down; let the salt scatter on to paper covered with wallpaper paste. Make sure that the squeezy bottle is just free of the paper before swinging it gently.

Use a stop-watch to time various activities: how long it takes everyone to change for PE, to hop, skip or jump the length of the playground, to tie a shoelace, to write their name 20 times. How long does it take to pass a parcel round a circle of children? The first person to start holds the stop-watch.

Do fast and slow activities in PE. How many bunny hops can you do in ten seconds? Set up a simple fitness circuit and see how many of each exercise you can do before the sand runs out.

How many times does your pulse beat in a minute? Put a drawing pin on your wrist where your pulse is, and balance a straw on the pin to show your pulse beat. Use your pulse to time how long it takes your partner to walk down the corridor.

Draw or paint pictures of the main events in the school day, then put them in order. Make a chart to show the cycle of a school year. Make a timeline of time through the ages.

Investigate the history of telling the time at sea. Find out why keeping track of a ship's longitude was such a problem, whereas latitude could be calculated by the sun. Find out about John Harrison (1693–1776) and his four ship's timers.

Toys

see also: Kaleidoscope, Transport

Experiment with a balloon. Draw a design on it and see what happens as you blow it up. Now do the same in reverse. Use a balloon to make a moving toy. Blow the balloon up and release it to make the toy move. Fix the balloon to a stretched string with a straw to make it shoot off in a straight line. How can

you make the balloon release air more slowly?

Choose a soft toy and make a book about it: its portrait, information on its height, weight and waist measurement, a made-up story about it. Make a simple garment for it.

Test-fly paper aeroplanes in the hall or in the playground. How far can you get them to fly? Can you make one that will carry a marble or a plastic cube?

Make a boat that floats. Investigate how to make it move faster in the water: adjusting the shape, adding sails, streamlining the design, adding a motor, or a paddle driven by a rubber band.

Make a moving toy with a spring. Use a rubber band and a cotton reel, or a squeezy bottle, and other bits and pieces. How fast will the toy go? How far will it go with 20 winds, or 40 winds? Does it go in a

straight line, or in a circle? Can it pull a load up a ramp?

Draw a plan of each floor of the dolls' house. Each group takes a room, and marks on the plan where to put furniture. Make some simple furniture from old matchboxes, cotton reels and bottle tops. Make wallpaper for the house with a repeating pattern. Make a brick wallpaper for the outside.

Fold a strip of paper into a concertina and cut out a string of paper dolls (or trees, flowers, cars).

Explore how much of a person's height is taken up by their head, legs or bodies. Is it the same with soft toys and dolls? Compare how the doll's legs and arms move with your own. What other differences are there?

Trails

see also: Geography, Maps, Outings, Vertical and pp 28–29

A Maths Trail can help you to make mathematical connections that no-one has noticed. Avoid counting and calculating for the sake of it, and look for clues that tell you why a particular feature is important. The shapes, for example, may have been used for structural reasons. Or the measurements may be standard because of the way that building materials are made.

Devise a simple Maths Trail around your school and the grounds.

Devise a Maths Trail for the Town Hall or a notable civic building. Focus on architectural details and the scale of these to see what makes a building 'grand'.

Collaborate with the local library or museum to create a Maths Trail locally. Scan in photos of significant features on the way. Link it to history or science or literature. Display it afterwards or run off copies for public use.

Create a Maths Trail for a local common or park. Include questions about the environment.

Transport

see also: Maps, Surveys, Toys

Visit a transport museum or pay attention to the vehicles you see at whatever outing you go on. How old are the vehicles? What purpose did (do) they serve? How many people do they carry? Record your data in a table.

Investigate toy cars. Which one rolls fastest down a slope? How can you make sure that your test is fair?

Investigate what factors seem to affect a vehicle's speed? Weight? The surface? The degree of slope?

Make (in pairs or teams) a vehicle that can carry a mass of 500 g. How does it move? On wheels, on water, like a sledge?

Estimate how far you walk in a normal day.

Draw in detail a bicycle wheel. Talk about symmetry.

Draw a picture of one tricycle. Use the computer or a photocopier to create two tricycles, three

tricycles… record the numbers of wheels. Use this display to help you learn your 3 times table.

Trees

see also: Environment, Gardening, Playground, Up, Vertical

There's always a tree or two somewhere near a school. Mathematical explorations of trees generally involve measurement and data handling.

Find out what kind of tree it is. How do we classify trees? What are the significant features of a tree that make it one species rather than another?

Collect leaves and classify them.

Make bark rubbings.

Look at the outline of the trees in summer and in winter.

Plant a tree to celebrate an event, or to celebrate the Maths Week. Plan the planting, working out the

size of the hole needed for the size of the tree, the quantity of water to moisten the soil, the tools needed, the length of the stake to hold it in place, and so on. Once it's planted, record its height and girth, and continue to record these every year to chart its progress. Plan a timetable of after-care for the tree, such as watering, feeding, pruning, staking.

Make a classification chart of the trees around the school, so that everyone can identify them.

Collect different methods for finding the height of a tree. Try them out. See if they give similar and sensible results. Make posters describing the different methods so that others can understand and use them.

Plot all the trees in your local area on a map. Invent a tree trail, with clues about the trees on the trail.

Use felled trees to work out their age. Decide other

methods of working out the age of a tree: measure the girth, look at the height, count the branches.

Look at samples of different wood. Why are some woods called 'soft wood' and others called 'hard wood'? Find out about wood that is used in making different furniture. Write descriptions of wood that will help identify beech or elm or mahogany in furniture.

Investigate a tree, or group of trees, in your playground, park or street. Record the kind of tree, and how many there are. Find out their approximate ages: a tree grows roughly 2·5 centimetres in girth (circumference) each year, so measure the girth of the tree to the nearest centimetre about 1·5 metres from the ground, divide by

2·5 and you have the approximate age of the tree. Now work out the average age of the trees. Find out what was happening in your area when these trees were planted. Who might have planted them, and why?

Design a tree skeleton using Logo. Define a programme for making each new branch and set of twigs.

U

Universe

see also: Infinity

Exploring the mathematics of the universe gives an opportunity to discuss extremely large numbers. For example, light travels through space at a speed of about 300 000 kilometres

each second. A light year is the distance light travels in a year, which is about 9·5 million million kilometres. The sun is 150 million kilometres away, which is eight light minutes.

Create a visual means of conveying the enormity of one million. Look at the visual clues in the book *How much is a million?* (David M Schwartz), which includes pages showing one million stars.

Look up to the sky. Find out about distances to the planets and the stars. Scientists use metric measures for astronomic lengths. A million metres is a megametre. A thousand megametres is a gigametre, and a thousand of these is a terrametre. The star Antares is 3·8 million terrametres from earth.

Unknown

see also: Logic, Problems and puzzles

The unknown is a mathematical term for the

term in an algebraic equation whose value has not yet been worked out.

Hold an Unknown workshop for Year 6 children and assist them in discovering the unknown by solving algebraic equations, such as:

$$x + 1 = 5$$
$$x + 3 = 15 - 5$$
$$y = x + 1$$
$$2a = 6$$
$$120/b = 12$$

Use an empty box to represent the unknown with younger children.

$$\square + 4 = 14$$
$$13 \times \square = 130$$

Up

see also: Trees, Vertical

Make an instrument to measure the height of something. Measure how high your school is, and your classroom. Find a tall tree and measure its height.

Go to the playground. Climb up something. Now jump down or slide down. How long did it take you to go up? How long did it take you to come down? Time yourself. Try it five times and see if the times change.

Invite someone to play a kazoo or piano or comb-and-paper. Find a way of telling them whether to play higher or lower notes. Can you write down symbols to show them what to play?

How far up the (outside) school wall can you bounce a ball? How can you measure the distance?

How far up in the air can you throw a ball? Can you measure or estimate the distance?

How far up in the air can you stretch your arms and hands?

Explore opposites. What is the opposite of 'up'? What other opposite pairs are there?

Discuss what might be happening 100 metres up in the air. And 100 metres below the ground. What about 500 metres or a kilometre? What about 100 kilometres?

Make up a game that involves a vertical number line, where players move

counters up and down the line. If you included negative numbers you could go down below zero – under the ground, maybe.

V

U
V

Vedic mathematics

Chinese mathematics, Greek mathematics, Egyptian mathematics

Vedic mathematics is the name given to an ancient system of mental calculation that was created by mathematicians in India and is still used by people all round the world who want to work out sums fast in their head.

Use the Vedic sutras or rules to do all your calculations during Maths Week.

Vegetables

see also: Café, Cooking, Food, Gardening, Weighing

Display a collection of vegetables, and use it as a

starting point for some **mathematical activities.**

Do a survey of people's most favourite and least favourite vegetables. Draw up a chart of your findings.

Cook a selection of recipes using vegetables during the Week.

Prepare and serve crunchy vegetables with dips:

1. cut florets of cauliflower and broccoli

2. make carrot and celery sticks

3. mix together yoghurt, sour cream, honey and a little barbecue sauce

4. dip and eat.

Prepare and serve crunchy vegetable pancakes:

1. make a pancake mixture

2. cook some savoury pancakes

3. shred carrots and lettuce

4. chop peppers and tomatoes finely

5. grate some cheese

6. arrange all these on the pancakes

7. season and add some mayonnaise

8. roll up each pancake and eat.

Cook a vegetable stir fry with chopped garlic, ginger and spring onions, beanshoots or Chinese tinned mushrooms, sliced red pepper, and some Chinese cabbage. Be careful: the oil needs to be pretty hot before you add the ingredients. Add soy sauce and, if you want to, some black bean sauce or a bit of hoisin sauce. Time how long you cook everything in the wok or pan. Keep it short, so that the vegetables stay quite crunchy.

Sort out a tray of vegetables in different ways. Find out which part of the plant the vegetable is: the root, the stalk, the fruit.

Find out the percentage of water in various different vegetables, and identify the vitamins contained in them.

Set up a market stall with real or play vegetables.

Research the function of garlic in Chinese, Mediterranean and other diets. What are its medicinal properties? Does it have to be cooked before you can eat it? What climate conditions does it need to grow well? Produce a poster describing ten things you can do with garlic.

Cut vegetables open and draw the cross-section. Make vegetable prints. Describe the shapes you see, and look for symmetry.

Cook barbecued or grilled sweetcorn with melted butter. Write down a recipe for others to copy. Include the timings.

Choose your own favourite vegetable recipe. Write it out. Produce a class recipe book for vegetables. Then move on to fruits…

Organise a vegetable tasting session and find out who likes what.

Research the history of vegetables and make a vegetable discovery timeline.

Vertical

see also: Architecture, Trees, Up

Collect examples of objects that are vertical and horizontal.

Make a simple balance bar with a strip of wood such as an old ruler, and hang it on a string loop so that it hangs level.

Make a clinometer with a straw, a protractor and a plumb bob, to find the height of trees and buildings.

Walk around the school environment with a home-made plumb line (tie something heavy on to the end of a long piece of string). Make a spirit level

with a plastic tube filled with water and a cork at each end. Use the trapped air bubble to show whether a surface is horizontal. Sketch your findings.

Victorians

see also: History

Any historical period will yield scope for practice in mathematical skills.

Design a timeline of key events and inventions in the reign of Victoria, to display in the classroom or the hall.

Find out statistics about the population.

For example, when Victoria became queen, the population of Britain was about 20 million, and about 20 per cent of people lived in towns and cities. By the end of her reign, the population was about 40 million and about 75 per cent of people lived in towns and cities.

Compare a weekly Victorian shopping bill with one today. Note any differences, such as paying for servants and coal rather than electric appliances.

Find out about weekly income for different kinds of work. Compare working conditions.

Do a survey of popular Victorian first names, and a survey of popular names in the school.

Find out if you could squeeze up a chimney to sweep it.

Vikings

see also: History

The activities suggested here could be applied to any historical period.

Find out how far the Viking invasions stretched throughout the world. Show this on a map and work out the distance.

Investigate the measures used by the Vikings, and their equivalents in metric units.

Explore the braid patterns used by the Vikings and invent similar ones.

Make a Viking tunic. How much material will you need? What shape will you need to cut out?

Design a symmetrical shield in the Viking style.

Find out the dimensions of Viking longships, and the number of oarsmen arranged in them. Draw a Viking longship.

Plan and carry out a trip to a museum to look at its Viking collection.

Visitors

see also: Books, Café, Competitions

Visitors introduce fresh thinking and ideas to the children and can reinforce links between school and community. Not all visitors will be experienced in talking with schoolchildren: offer help beforehand.

Invite people to come in and talk about how they use numeracy in their job. (The website that was originally set up for Maths Year 2000, www.counton. org, contains a wide sample of individuals in different jobs, giving a brief account of the importance of mathematics in their careers.)

Invite the librarian to visit and talk about the changing role of libraries and about the need for numeracy in a librarian's job.

Ask a cook, chef or baker to come in and tell children about their job and the mathematical components of it. Extend it to a hands-on workshop.

Ask someone who owns or works in a café or restaurant to visit. (You can combine these visits with a café run by the children and an outing to a shop or café.)

Invite someone who works in the media to talk about the importance of accurate timing.

Open your doors to parents, to offer help or participate in a workshop, an open evening or any maths activity.

Volume

see also: Size, Water, Weighing, You

Hold a volume and capacity workshop.

Pack and unpack a suitcase. See how much

you can fit in with careful packing.

How many tiny things can you fit into a matchbox?

Estimate, then find out how many potatoes you can fit into the saucepan of water before it overflows.

Make a box using Lego which will hold just 20 marbles, or 20 pencils.

Find out whose hand has the greatest capacity.

Cut the top off a plastic bottle. Mark a level and pour in water to below that level. Decide which objects (a stone, a potato, a ball, a conker, a cork…) will make the water reach that level.

Find out who has the largest fist by submerging your fist in water.

Find the volume of an egg.

Make a cube from linking cubes. Find its volume and surface area. Make another cube with doubled dimensions. Find its volume and surface area.

What is the capacity of your lungs?

Produce a chart for converting Imperial measures of capacity to metric.

W

Walks

see also: Games, Trails, x-axis

A maths walk need not follow a prescribed route nor have the set tasks of a Maths Trail. It is therefore open to interpretation and, to some extent, serendipity.

Take with you a set of Instructions cards. Every time you stop, invite someone to pick a card and follow the Instruction, such as 'add 100 to the number of the house nearest you' or 'measure round the next lamp-post'.

Go for a walk in a park. Take your sketchbooks. Stop at places to make drawings that recreate the scene or object in the form of angles, or shapes or symmetry.

Walk from school to the library (or other nearby building, such as leisure centre or bus station). How can you measure the distance?

Water

see also: Environment, Geography, Vegetables, Volume, Weather

During the Maths Week you can organise facilities for exploration of water for all ages, inside and outside. Use plain water, warm water, foam, coloured water, ice cubes, baking soda (to make it fizz). Provide a variety of equipment, selecting a few at a time for a particular purpose. Have mops, buckets and cloths to hand.

Use floating foam numbers, and have a

surface to stick them on when wet. Put plastic counting books and toys in the water.

Set up a hairdresser's shop with suitable dolls and pretend equipment.

Freeze coloured water in jelly moulds and ice trays. Encapsulate small toys. Float them, turn them out, watch them melt.

Combine water with different ingredients, using food colouring, containers and plastic syringes.

Put holes in plastic containers and bags in different ways. Explore the sprays and jets.

Be decorators (outdoors), and paint the walls with water using decorating brushes and rollers. First,

measure and divide the wall into sections (use fractions). Working in teams, estimate how long it will take a team to paint one section. Then do the work and check your time against your estimate. Now try again: before you start, discuss what you can do to make your time faster.

Organise an apple bobbing event. Count how many times it takes you to put your head in the water before you catch the apple.

Organise a paddling pool event, well supervised.

Work out how much water you use a day, a week, a year for everything you do and need.

Investigate how much water you have in your body. What does it mean to become dehydrated? How can you stop that from happening?

Find out how you can get water up from a well. Design your own well. Draw a diagram, marking on it how the different parts of your design work.

Weather

see also: Environment, Geography, Surveys

Design and make a wind machine.

Design and make devices for measuring rainfall, wind speed, wind direction…

Look for evidence of wind. Hold up a wet finger. Find clues (plants moving, paper blowing along, washing on the line). Look at the clouds moving.

Measure the wind force.

Investigate meteorological websites on the Internet. How do they get their information? What is the weather like today? And in Florence? And Addis Ababa? In Shanghai? In New York? Kentucky? Durham? Edinburgh?… Draw a map of all or part of the world and mark on it the weather different areas are having today.

Survey the weather (rain, wind, sun) hour by hour. Put the results into a weather book.

Learn how to read a maximum/minimum thermometer.

How many inches of rain fell in the first week of this month? And in the first week of November?

V
W

Compare this with Kendal in Cumbria. Produce a chart showing rainfall over the last three or five years.

Investigate how and why water turns to ice.

Why does it rain? What happens when a river floods? Look up past accounts. What can be done to prevent damage from flooding (or to prevent flooding)? Investigate flooding in other parts of the world.

Weaving

see also: Design and technology, Patterns

Weaving patterns have an underlying system or procedure that is mathematical. At its most simple, the pattern is ABAB, or 'odd, even, odd, even'. Professional weavers use complex mathematics.

Invite a professional weaver into the school for the week to work with the children. Or organise a visit to a weaver. Investigate

the mathematics in their planning.

Do paper weaving by cutting a curved warp, and weaving in straight weft strips of paper in different colours. Fold the paper over and cut, making a symmetrical warp.

Make a simple card loom.

Analyse weaving patterns to find out the basic pattern. Record it as u (under) and o (over), for example ouoouoouoouo.

Display a range of weaving: basket weaving, woven artefacts, ikat weaving, rugs, carpets, belts, and so on.

Weave polygons on a circular paper plate, with the warp cut into the plate, and the weft woven round. Make a hexagon. Then try a pentagon.

Weave ribbon on railings outside.

Weighing

see also: Physical maths, Volume

Hold a weighing workshop.

Choose a shoe. Find objects which are lighter, heavier, about the same.

Weigh a pumpkin on bathroom scales. Work out how many pumpkins weigh the same as you.

Find out if you would be able to pick up a bag containing 50 000 paper clips.

Hide different things in yoghurt pots with lids. Challenge your partner to put the pots in order of weight.

Guess the weights of each of the balls in the tray.

Estimate how many conkers will balance the melon. Or how much water will balance the doll.

Set out a collection of groceries weighing one kilogram.

Set up a display of weighing apparatus, old and new.

Find the weight of honey contained in the jar.

Make a chart that converts Imperial measures of weight to metric.

Investigate the weights of boxers: flyweight, bantamweight, lightweight, and so on.

Explore unusual measurements of weight. Diamonds are weighed in carats. A carat was the weight of a grain of corn, now set at one fifth of a gram. Women's stockings and tights are measured in denier, which is a measurement of weight. Ten denier tights are made from a yarn that weighs ten grams for every 9000 metres of yarn. A bushel measured the weight of grains of oats, barley and wheat.

Find out the difference between weight and mass.

Make an egg-weight cake. Balance an egg first with flour, then with butter, then with sugar. Mix all these together, and enough milk to make a cake. Cook for

20 minutes in a moderate oven.

Are you worth your weight in gold?

Compare a selection of kitchen scales. How accurate are they?

Woodwork

see also: Construction, Design and technology, Shapes, Trees

Woodwork activities will reinforce children's appreciation of the properties of shape. When you teach children how to use wood-working tools, include a discussion on the angle at which chisels and cutters are used and how to use set squares and tapes to measure length and angle. Arrange adult support for any woodworking sessions.

Ask a carpenter to come into school and demonstrate their craft.

Assemble a 3D abstract artwork inside picture frames by using offcuts of wood. Use a range of different sized frames and different types and sizes of wood to compose the picture. Provide a title and commentary with each picture, describing the amount of wood used and the way it was assembled.

Explore wood sculpture by carving out shapes from logs or redundant tree branches. Display the sculptures together with the shapes that have been chiselled out of the logs.

Cut different lengths of bamboo sticks and string together to make wind chimes and suspend as many as possible outside to make a gigantic wind chime.

X-axis

Have fun with coordinates.

Play battleships.

Bury treasure and mark it on a grid. Use coordinate clues to find it.

Mark a simple grid on the sand tray with string, and give clues about where the hidden toy is.

Draw a picture using coordinates in all four quadrants. Challenge a partner to draw the picture using the coordinate references you supply.

Go orienteering locally, using grid-map references.

Draw a simple picture on a square grid. Now reproduce the picture twice the size on another grid. Use a skewed grid to make a skewed copy. Use a wavy grid, a short grid, a tall grid, a graduated grid...

X-rays

Look at how x-rays are used to see bones and other hard matter in the human body. How many bones are there in your hand? In your feet? In your whole body? Which part of

---

your body has the most bones? Which is the longest bone? The shortest? What would you do without bones?

Make a plaster of Paris model of your teeth. Use new, clean playdoh as a mould, and bite into it. How many teeth have you got? Have you got all your teeth yet? Why does the dentist sometimes do an x-ray of people's teeth?

Make full-size skeletons matching your own body measurements, using strips of tough paper or card. Now make a skeleton that is half your size. Or make one a quarter your size, or one tenth your size.

How much skin do you have? Make an outline of all your skin using centimetre-squared paper.

Y

You

The starting points are limitless for a project on the

---

children themselves. The mathematics will mainly be measuring and data handling, but other aspects will emerge as children raise more questions.

Names: How many times can you write your name in two minutes? Would you expect the answer to be the same for Samantha and Zoë? How many letters are there in your name? What length of name is most common?

Bodies: Investigate your lung capacity. Design and make a belt to fit yourself. How far can you hear? How many children can fit on a PE mat? How much water do you drink in a day? How much should you drink in a day? How do you keep your balance?

Hands: How many counters can you hold in your hand? Does your left hand hold as much as your right hand? What is the surface area of your palm? Your whole hand? Who has the biggest hand?

Fingers: Collect some long thin things (pencils, string, felt-tipped pens, pipe cleaners, a candle) and compare their widths to your finger. How long is each finger? Is the second finger always the longest? How strong is your finger? How long can you hold up a book in the air? Take your fingerprints. Decide what prints you have: whorl, loop, arch or composite. Are they all the same, or do they vary? Can you identify the fingerprints of other people?

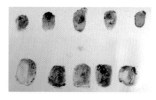

Touch: Put different fabrics and papers in a feely bag (velvet, sandpaper, tissue paper, plastic or silk) and see if you can identify them all.

Feet: Is the person with the longest foot the tallest? Find out which of your toes is the longest. Does your right foot have the same area as your left foot? How many socks are there in the room today? Make footprints with paint on paper. Can you tell whose foot belongs to whom? Shut your eyes and feel different papers and fabrics with your toes. Can you tell them apart?

Motion: How high can you jump? Put ink on your fingers and jump up and touch the paper on the wall to find out. Can you do 100 skips? How long does it take? Make up a dance involving a certain number of hops, skips and jumps; describe it to your partner or write down the sequence for the group you are in.

Clothes: Investigate clothes fastenings. What kinds are there? What kinds are represented in the class today? Design an outfit

for yourself using different patterns, or symmetry.

Age: If you added together the ages of the people in your class, what would the total be? Could someone be that old? Make a timeline of your life so far.

Television: What are your favourite TV programmes? How much (on a scale of zero to 10) do you like them? Do the same for the programmes you really do not like. Use this data to produce a chart that reflects the likes and dislikes of the class.

Zeno's paradox

see also: Greek mathematics, Infinity

Older children can tackle mathematical magic and puzzles and teasers, and try

and unravel their meaning. Zeno's paradox is one of these.

To find 3 by 3 Middle number in 5 And a by 4 in 6, 8, 9, 11 And Edge of the Magic squares has even number and in between has add number

Zeno was a Greek philosopher of 5 BCE, and he used the parable of Achilles and the tortoise. He argued that a traveller walking to a specific destination will never get there because the traveller must first walk half the distance. At the halfway point, the traveller will then have to walk half the remaining distance. Then half of the half that remains. Since there will always be half of the remaining part to walk, and an infinite number of halfway points, the traveller will never arrive.

Zero

see also: Calculators, Infinity, Number lines and tracks

Collect words that mean nothing: zero, nought, zilch, nada, niente, empty, absence, vacuum, love, duck, nil… Discuss where and when these words are used.

Make up calculations with zero as the answer.

Make up divisions that give the remainder zero.

$$4 \div 2 = 2 \, r \, 0$$
$$42 \div 6 = 7 \, r \, 0$$

Research the history of zero. Find out when zero was first used in Europe, and then when it was finally taken on in Britain.

Investigate how the Romans tackled zero.

Explore what happens on a calculator when you add zero, subtract zero, multiply by zero and divide by zero. Talk about the meanings of these operations.

What is the point of zero? Discuss.

y
z

BEAM resources

The following resources may prove useful in a Maths Week and are all available from BEAM on 01242 267 945 or at www.beam.co.uk. BEAM consultants can run in-service training sessions on planning a Maths Week.

Books
The BEAM Book Basket

Family
Maths and Your Child
Maths Together

Games
board games and dice
Calculating Dominoes
card games
Domino Puzzles
dominoes
Essential Maths Workout
Gather Round Number Games
loop card games
Mad about Maths: mathematical games
mathematical games books
Mission Maths game and CD-ROM
number accessories
Number Challenge board games
spinners

ICT
overhead projector resources

Investigations, problems and puzzles
Big Numbers
Brain Buster Maths Box
mental mathematics flipbooks
puzzle books
Sums for Smart Kids
Teaching Mental Strategies
The Times File

Magic
Mad about Maths: number magic

Money
Colossal Cards
Mega Money
Money Counts

Music
Maths Raps
Hip Hop Times Table CD

Number lines and tracks
number lines and tracks
Using Number Lines with 5–8 year olds

Physical maths
Big Outdoor Maths Box

Reflection
mirrors
mirror books

Shapes
geostrips
Mad about Maths: shape and space
pattern blocks
Poleidoblocs

and for the whole **Maths Week** a maths resources pack